GOD
FOR US

OTHER BOOKS BY JAMES W. GILLEY

God With Us: According to John
Keep On Keeping On
The Battle Is the Lord's

GOD FOR US

According to John

KATA IΩANNHN

John 13–21

JAMES W. GILLEY

3ABN Books
PO Box 220
West Franklin, Illinois 62896
www.3ABN.org

Pacific Press® Publishing Association
Nampa, Idaho
Oshawa, Ontario, Canada
www.pacificpress.com

Cover design by Steve Lanto
Cover art resources from iStockphoto.com
Inside design by Aaron Troia

The author assumes full responsibility for the accuracy of all facts and quotations as cited in this book.

Unless otherwise noted, all Bible verses are from the New King James Version, copyright © 1979, 1980, 1982 Thomas Nelson, Inc., Publishers.

Scripture quotations marked KJV are from the King James Version.

Scripture quotations marked NIV are from the HOLY BIBLE, NEW INTERNATIONAL VERSION®. Copyright © 1973, 1978, 1984 by International Bible Society. Used by permission of Zondervan Publishing House. All rights reserved.

3ABN BOOKS is dedicated to bringing you the best in published materials consistent with the mission of Three Angels Broadcasting Network. Our goal is to uplift Jesus Christ through books, audio, and video materials by our family of 3ABN presenters. Our in-depth Bible study guides, devotionals, biographies, and lifestyle materials promote whole person health and the mending of broken people. For more information, call 618-627-4651 or visit 3ABN's Web site: www.3ABN.org.

Additional copies of this book are available from two locations:
3ABN: Call 1-800-752-3226 or visit http://www.3abn.org
Adventist Book Centers: Call toll-free 1-800-765-6955
or visit http://www.adventistbookcenter.com.

ISBN 13: 978-0-8163-2426-2
ISBN 10: 0-8163-2426-3

10 11 12 13 14 • 5 4 3 2 1

DEDICATION

Dedicated to our son,
John, and his lovely wife, Jerica,
that they might continue
to have the joy of Jesus and forever know
the One who is "the Way, the Truth, and the Life."

ACKNOWLEDGEMENTS

I owe a debt of gratitude to Dale Galusha and Jerry Thomas for encouraging me to write each of the books I have written and getting me started writing in the first place. My thanks to Russ Holt for the rush job he did in getting this manuscript ready for the press. To Kathy Smith and Diane Hamilton for typing the manuscripts and to Roy Thurmon and my loving wife, Camille, for reading each chapter and offering suggestions. To each of you my heartfelt thanks!

Contents

INTRODUCTION

A number of years ago, I was conducting evangelistic meetings in the Houston, Texas, area, when a motorcycle gang starting coming to the meetings each night! The first night that they came roaring into the parking lot, I can tell you, it alarmed some of the church members! They were sure the bikers were planning to disrupt the meetings. But they soon learned that these young men had recently become interested in the Bible, and some of them eventually gave their hearts to the Lord.

One night after the meeting, the leader of the motorcycle gang told me that the group intended to become a Christian motorcycle gang and that they were looking for a new name. I suggested the "Sons of Thunder," thinking of the way the Bible describes James and John, two of Christ's closest disciples. My suggestion struck a chord, and a few nights later, the gang showed up at the meetings with "Sons of Thunder" proudly displayed in large red letters across the backs of their black leather motorcycle jackets.

Mark 3:17 records Jesus giving James and John this title—"Sons of Thunder." John, whose Gospel we will be looking at in this book, was a child of the storm. He had a volatile spirit. He reacted to the challenges of life with vigor. He was very ambitious. Scripture reveals a far different figure than Leonardo da Vinci portrayed John to be in his immortal painting of the Last Supper. The artist pictures a soft, delicate, quiet, almost effeminate John—nothing at all like the portrait painted in the Gospels.

In the Gospels, we see a fiery young man who asks Jesus to let him call down fire from heaven to destroy the Samaritan village that denies them entrance. We see John wanting Christ to repudiate those who are casting out demons in Christ's name without proper authorization. We see a young man who came to Jesus with his mother; she requests that He place her sons on His right and left hand when He sets up His earthly kingdom.

But, you know, God can use a man like that! God can use a Son of Thunder. God would rather have a steamship that is plowing through the ocean off course than a drifting hulk of steel that is floating without power. He can redirect the path of the one who is off course, but He can't do much with one who is drifting aimlessly. He says He would wish that we were hot or cold rather than lukewarm (see Revelation 3:15, 16). God is disgusted with a church or a person that is like the English lord who said, "Any kind of religion will do for me just so it is cool and comfortable, and I can take it easy." If your faith lulls you to sleep and doesn't stir you to action, it is not the kind of message that John received from Jesus.

Primarily because of his writings, John has become so influential in Christianity that perhaps more young Christian men have been named John than any other name. The impact of many of them—for example, John Huss, John

Calvin, John Knox, John Weymouth, John Milton, John Bunyan, and John Wesley—has been felt around the world. As a child, I coveted the name John. My grandfather's name was John Robert, and my older brother was named after him. His son and grandson carry the same name. My father's name was John Wesley Gilley. I remember as a kid once asking my dad why he hadn't named me after him, why he hadn't named me John. As I mentioned, I already had an older brother named John, but at nine years old, I didn't see a problem with having more than one John in the family! This was before George Foreman, a heavyweight boxing champion, named all of his sons George, simply adding a number after each one's name! My dad tried to comfort me by reminding me that he and I had the same initials—J. W. and that I could be J. W. Jr. So for a few days, I went by J. W., but it just wasn't the same as John! John is a strong name for a strong disciple.

When we read John's Gospel, we are reading a book that has been read by more people than any other book in the history of the world. The first fourteen verses of the first chapter have often been called the greatest literature that has ever been written. It is written by one of the great minds of history, yet these great thoughts are written in very simple Greek. In spite of the simple language, nowhere can you find greater, more profound truths. When you read John, you are seeing the mind of his Teacher, Jesus. You find in the pages of John's Gospel, a presentation of the Deity.

In Matthew, we see Jesus as the *King*. Mark shows us Jesus as the *Servant*. Dr. Luke shows us Jesus as the quintessential *Man*. But John shares with us the truth that Jesus is *God*. More than any other Gospel writer, John shows us what God is like in the Person of Jesus.

A group of people were discussing the God of the Old Testament and how it often seemed that He was brutal and brought about so much bloodshed. A young girl, who was listening, said, "But that was before God became a Christian." We smile at this response, but if we had only the Old Testament, it might be difficult to get an accurate picture of God. Jesus came to this earth to give us salvation, but in doing so, He also showed us what God is like. By seeing Jesus, we see the Father.

The point that John makes over and over is that Jesus is God—God in human flesh. A God born into an ordinary family in an ordinary home, not in a palace as a king. A God who worked as a carpenter, who had probably hit His fingernail with a hammer and knew the struggles of an ordinary person. A God who knew what temptation was, yet who never sinned. A God who demonstrated that He could return hate with a love so strong that He was willing to die on a cross for you and me and all of humankind.

This is the picture of God that John gives us as he tells us about Jesus, who took on human form and came to live with us and to die for us. John knew this Jesus intimately. John was there at His baptism. He was at Cana and saw Jesus turn the water into wine. He was the only Gospel writer who personally witnessed the early Judean ministry. He was there for the resurrection of Lazarus. He was present at all the miracles, including the feeding of the five thousand. He was at Jesus' trial before Caiaphas; he was at the Crucifixion; he was the first to believe that Jesus had risen from the tomb. He was there, and he says that it is his desire that you believe these things as he believed them. In summing up his Gospel, he said, "These [things] are written that you may believe that Jesus is the Christ, the Son of

God, and that believing you may have life in His name" (John 20:31).

John makes it clear that it is vital that we believe in order to receive life eternal. He uses the word *believe* seventy times in his Gospel. What does it mean to believe? First of all, it means that you are convinced in your mind that Jesus is the Christ, the Son of God. There will be many times that Satan will use people and events to try to destroy that belief, and there may be many times that you will have to pray, " 'Lord, I believe; help my unbelief!' " (Mark 9:24). Second, it means that you trust that everything Christ has said is true. I often tell those who are seeking truth to get a red-letter edition of the Bible—one that prints the words of Jesus in red—and to simply "read the red."

If you will commit your life to those two things—to the person of Christ and to His Word—He will come and live in your heart. He will save you, and you will spend eternity with Him. My heart is warm as I thrill all over again at John's picture of the One who said, " 'I am the way, the truth, and the life' " (John 14:6).

So, let's look together at the last half of John's Gospel and see the picture he paints of Jesus.

VOLUME II

Chapter 1 — John 13

ATTRIBUTES OF A TRUE DISCIPLE

It was a very cold day, to say the least. Rain was falling, and the temperature kept dropping until it was below fifteen degrees Fahrenheit. Add to that the Texas wind and the ice that was forming, and it was definitely a good day to be indoors by a fireplace with a good book! But we were not indoors. We were bivouacking with the Medical Cadet Corps (MCC) in a remote area near Lake Whitney, some twenty-five miles from the campus of what is now Southwestern Adventist University. Some of you may not know what the MCC was. During the days when the military draft was still in effect in our country, the Medical Cadet Corps was an integral part of Seventh-day Adventist education for academy- and college-aged males. It combined medical and first-aid instruction with military training, and it almost guaranteed that Adventist young men who had gone through the MCC would be assigned to be a medic if drafted into the United States Army. And that was a great place for a Sabbath keeper.

Captain Clyde Carlton "C. C." Blackburn, a World War II veteran and the director of the Medical Cadet Corps at

Southwestern Adventist University, was very serious about MCC training. Those who served in the MCC under him later reported that they did very well when they put that knowledge into practice in the United States Army. In fact, some of them said that the MCC was tougher than army basic training!

Twice a year, we went on bivouac. This was a chance to put all that we had learned in our Tuesday night sessions into practice in an actual field situation. Bivouacking was like a test and how we handled it had a lot to do with our MCC grade.

With the weather like it was, we thought that surely "Captain" (as we affectionately called Captain Blackburn) would cancel the outing, but he had no intention of doing such a thing. I was the first sergeant of the corp, so Cadet Major Jim Hoehn (later to become president of the Kansas-Nebraska Conference) took me along with him to Captain's headquarters tent and told him that the troops were cold and wet and that we were afraid we were going to have a lot of sick fellows on our hands if we stayed at the campsite. Captain explained to us that hardships were part of training and that this was a great opportunity to test our ability to cope with difficult situations. As the three of us talked it over, Captain shared some ideas and suggestions and then left it to us to solve the situation. By the way, that was great training!

Cadet Major Hoehn and I talked some more, and then Jim returned to the officers' quarters. I went to the campsite where there were 180 cadets waiting, expecting to hear that we were breaking camp and going home.

It was my responsibility to tell them that we were staying and to hear their groans and see the disappointed looks on their faces. I instructed them to take off their wet clothes and put on dry underwear—nothing but dry underwear! I told them that they would then be given a hot footbath while in their two-man pup tents, after which they were to get into their sleeping bags and not get out until the bugler sounded reveille the next morning.

One of the cadets who remembers that bivouac well is J. D. Quinn, head of the pastoral department at Three Angels Broadcasting Network and husband of Shelley Quinn, a well-known Bible teacher. Another is Max Trevino, president of the Southwestern Union Conference and a 3ABN board member.

With my assistant, Edwin Sharpe, who later became a pastor, I went to every tent, washing the cadets' feet as they stuck them out the flap of their tent. As I made sure those feet were very dry, I instructed each cadet that he was not to leave his ice-covered tent until morning and whatever he did, he was not to put his cold, wet clothes back on until morning. Extra underwear was the only clothing change each cadet had brought for the long weekend—Thursday through Sunday.

When morning came, 179 cadets of the 180 came forth from a good night's sleep. One cadet had either failed to hear my instructions—or failed to follow them—and had spent a miserable night shivering in his wet clothes. That day the weather got so bad that Captain received permission from the property owner for us to move into a deserted old brick mansion nearby. We slept there the next two nights and were dry at least but still cold!

Wherever I go, I run into men who were on that bivouac and remember that night vividly, even after so many years. They always mention the footbath! Now, I didn't wash those men's feet because of some great humility on my part, although washing someone's feet was not new to me, because our church practices the ordinance of humility—footwashing—as part of the Communion service. Nor did I wash their feet because I was trying to teach them humility by example. I washed their feet because I knew that it would help keep them warm, along with the dry underwear, and I didn't need a bunch of sick cadets on my hands with all of the drills and projects that Captain had planned for us. But whatever my reasons, over and over through the years, former cadets who were on that trip have told me how much they appreciated me washing their feet and how much comfort it brought them. They've described how they burrowed down in their sleeping bags for a cozy night's sleep after that warm footbath.

Of course, Jesus didn't wash the disciples' feet to keep them warm. He did it to teach them—and us—that greatness comes only to those who understand the true humility of service to others.

What He did was remarkable indeed. In that time and society, washing someone's feet was the work of a slave. For example, although many rabbis had disciples who would render personal service to them, a disciple would never dream of performing a service such as this. Washing feet was far beneath anyone except a slave. If you went to the home of someone who had no slave, then you washed your own feet when they had become dirty by walking along dusty roads, wearing only sandals. Today, we live in an antiseptic world; we Americans bathe daily. In many parts of the world, people laugh at us for this—even in parts of Europe! There a weekly bath is more the norm than a daily one and washing one's feet and a sponge bath under the arms is the daily practice. I've traveled in some parts of the world where I suspected that the custom was an *annual* bath or perhaps none at all!

As Jesus' disciples entered the room, they saw the pot with water, a basin for washing, and a towel for drying, but there was no servant present to take care of their needs. Perhaps they thought one was coming later; but one thing was certain: the thought of one of them performing the task for the others never entered their minds. Jesus had demonstrated the service of love throughout His ministry, yet they had missed most of what He taught and lived. There was a lot of contention between them: Who was the greatest? Who would be Jesus' second in command when He was ruling over Israel as they still expected Him to do?

At the table, John moved in on one side of Jesus and Judas on His other side. The disciples had been very upset when James and John had their mother ask Jesus to give them special positions of power when He came into His kingdom. Judas knew of the brothers' scheming; and even though he had already made arrangements to betray the Lord, he was keeping all of his options open. If he saw that Jesus had a great position for him, he could double-cross the Pharisees with whom he was dealing. There are even those who think that Judas was trying to force the hand of Christ and make Him show Himself as a military Messiah, who would restore Israel to prominence. One thing, however, is sure: Judas never once thought about washing anyone's feet. Neither did John or any of the other disciples, for that matter. They would wait for a servant to show up. But when one didn't, they were surprised to see the Lord get up, gird Himself with a towel, pour water from the pot to the basin, and begin to wash the disciples' feet, starting, some believe, with Judas.

When Jesus came to Peter, the impetuous disciple refused to let the Lord kneel before him. This is the man who first proclaimed that Jesus was truly the Son of God, the man who first really grasped the divinity of Christ. To have the Creator wash his feet was something he just could not see himself allowing. " 'You shall never wash my feet,' " Peter said; but the Lord answered, " 'If I do not wash you, you have no part with Me' " (John 13:8).

In that case Peter answered, " 'Lord, not my feet only, but also my hands and my head!' " (verse 9). The Lord dismissed this as unnecessary.

The ordinance of humility is a beautiful service that we Adventists do as a prelude to the Communion service itself. At one time, a number of denominations practiced footwashing, but only a few do so today. This service may seem a bit strange to someone who attends the quarterly Communion service for the first time. I remember taking a friend named Mack Hickman to church with me when I was about twelve years old. He was spending the weekend with our family while his parents were out of town. Not long ago, I heard from Mack, and he recalled going to church with me that Sabbath and having me wash his feet. He said it was the only time that anyone other than his mother had ever washed his feet. He said he had thought about it a number of times over the years, and later, as he studied the Bible for himself, he had seen the significance of the service.

Now, when Christ washed the disciples' feet, they were dirty! If there is ever a time that you want to make sure your feet are *not* dirty, it is when you go to an Adventist church on Communion Sabbath, which is often the thirteenth Sabbath, and participate in the ordinance of humility! In all the years that I have been participating in the foot-washing service, I have washed only one man's feet that were dirty enough to change the color of the water in the basin! Those feet really needed washing! So, why do we wash people's already clean feet? It's very simple. Jesus said, " 'I have given you an example, that you should do as I have done to you' " (verse 15). He wants us to learn and practice the principle of humility. I've had people tell me, "I would never wash someone's feet; do you think that it's really necessary for salvation?" To whom I would reply, "It might not be necessary for everyone, but for you it may be vital!" Why? Because there is something within us that needs to die. It's called pride, selfishness, or self-centeredness, and a good way to start killing it is by washing someone's feet. And if I am not willing to do this, which our Lord did, it means that there is a need in my life for humility. Pastor Hal Steenson speaks of this condition as "the addiction of pride." It's an addiction that is difficult to detect and even more difficult to eradicate from our lives.

Humility is such a tricky thing—or perhaps I should say that pride is so deceitful that unless we're careful, we can be proud of our humility! Pastor Ben Leach, one of my great mentors in life, used to say, "I recently wrote a book titled *Humility and How I Obtained It*. But when I finished writing it, the book was so good that pride entered my heart, and I had to destroy the manuscript because I had lost my humility!"

Pastor Leach enjoyed telling this humorous story, but he also knew that he was sharing a great truth: *when you think about humility and focus on it, you will lose it for sure.*

What you will be left with is a false humility that attempts to appear humble but really isn't. Forget about yourself, focus on Jesus and on others, and humility will fall into place by itself. Humility isn't something you can learn or develop. It's a natural by-product of really knowing Jesus and patterning your life after His—a life of service. By the way, when you do this, you will be so relaxed and secure that some people will think you don't have humility. But remember, the Lord knows your heart, and it's what *He* thinks that's important. Christ wants us to have a genuine humility, not a phony "poor me" kind of humility that tries to camouflage a deeper pride—an obsession with self, which is what pride really is.

The ordinance of humility is a good opportunity for a "humility check." If I find myself skipping that part of the service too often, I might need to ask myself, "Why?"

When I was president of the Arkansas-Louisiana Conference, the conference took our pastors to Israel on a study trip that most of them tell me they will never forget. While there, we arranged to have a short service in the traditional upper room where Jesus ate the Last Supper with His disciples. It is most likely on the very site where the original was located. When our group arrived, there was only a little bit of water, one basin, and a small towel. There were fifty of us, and the only way to carry out the ordinance of humility was for a couple of us to do all the washing of the feet. So Max Trevino and I began washing the feet of each person. It was a very simple, but a very beautiful, service. Before long, other tour groups, not familiar with the footwashing service as Adventists are, came into the room. Some asked if we would wash their feet, and we did. They mingled their tears with ours, and we all had a great spiritual time together.

Jesus said, " 'If I then, your Lord and Teacher, have washed your feet, you also ought to wash one another's feet' " (verse 14). Servanthood, serving others, is essential for a disciple of Jesus, and it comes only through true humility. Jesus says that if you want true happiness and blessing, you can find them through serving others. " 'If you know these things, blessed [some translations say "happy"] are you if you do them' " (verse 17).

The second essential for a disciple of Jesus that we find in John 13 is *loyalty.* As Jesus washed Judas's feet, it apparently was this disciple's last chance to confess his sin and to give his heart to the Lord. But instead of being drawn to Jesus by this act of humility, he hardened his heart. He saw Jesus' actions as weakness and concluded that Jesus could never be king of Israel and that betraying Him had been the right decision all along. He thought he might as well at least take the priests' thirty pieces of silver and get something out of this lost cause. Obviously, Jesus would never be king! Selfishness always leads to disloyalty of one kind or another. Perhaps Judas felt that he had been slighted in some way or that he had not received enough credit for his contributions to the cause. Whatever the reason, bitterness started building in his heart, and soon he found himself estranged from the Lord.

This didn't come as a surprise to Jesus. He said, " 'I tell you before it comes' " (verse 19), and then He described what was going to take place—that He would be betrayed by one in the group. That does not mean that Judas was predestined to do this and that he couldn't change his mind. It simply means that Jesus knew Judas so well that He knew his weakness and that it would lead him to betray Him.

Jesus had intentionally placed Judas in the position of

treasurer to take care of the group's money. Why? Perhaps because He knew that Judas was good at making and managing money. However, it's true that we are often most tempted in the areas in which we have the most ability. If you are very good at something, watch out and be very careful, because the devil may find it easy to trip you up in this very area. To paraphrase H. M. S. Richards Sr., the great preacher and founder of the Voice of Prophecy, "If a man is a better mechanic, architect, singer, or whatever than I am, that is not a problem. I'm not the least bit jealous." Then he went on to admit, "But if a man . . . can preach a better sermon than I can and do better on the radio than I can and beat me at my own job, then it takes the grace of God for me to really love him and praise him from the bottom of my heart."[1] So in all likelihood, the sphere of your greatest ability will be the area where you are most vulnerable and where the devil will tempt you. Judas was not only good with money, he *loved* money.

In addition, Judas was not a loyal person. Loyalty is a trait that is developed as we place the needs and feelings of others above our own and as we truly care whether our actions will hurt another, rather than being interested only for our own benefit. If our hearts are tender and sensitive to the Spirit of God, He will convict us when we are disloyal to God, a loved one, or a friend. If we will listen to the Holy Spirit, He will lead us to have true loyalty—not only to those about us but to God and His truth too.

God can take our failures—for instance, disloyalty—and turn them into our strengths, if we will let Him. He can make us into loyal people who can be trusted by God,

---

1. H. M. S. Richards Sr., *Feed My Sheep* (Washington, D.C.: Review and Herald® Publishing Association, 1958), 73, 74.

friends, and family! He could have done this for Judas, but Judas would not let Him. In fact, Judas could have changed his mind right down to the very end, but he didn't. And that night his name became synonymous with disloyalty, with being a traitor. Loyalty is an essential quality for a disciple of Jesus Christ.

John 13 mentions a third essential quality of a disciple, and that quality is love! John wrote, "So, when he [Judas] had gone out, Jesus said, 'Now the Son of Man is glorified, and God is glorified in Him. If God is glorified in Him, God will also glorify Him in Himself, and glorify Him immediately' " (verses 31, 32). These verses set the stage for what Christ will say about love.

Jesus has such a close relationship with His Father that He completely reflects the Father's character and His will. The Father and the Son are One, and because They are One, if One is glorified, Both are glorified.

Christ saw the coming cross not as a defeat, but rather as a complete victory over sin. He had predicted all along His death that was to come, but also He predicted His resurrection from the dead. When He said, " 'Destroy this temple, and in three days I will raise it up' " (John 2:19), He was, of course, speaking of His resurrection. He knew that after the Crucifixion He would rise again and ascend to the Father.

He obeyed the Father even unto the death of the cross, and obedience was the way that Jesus glorified the Father. Obedience through the indwelling of Christ through the Holy Spirit is the only way that our obedience brings glory to Him. When the devil is unable to get a person to deny God's existence, he does all he can to distort the person's discipleship—just as he did to Judas. Satan was successful in leading the Pharisees and the religious leaders of Christ's day into legalism. Today, however, his most successful ploy is to lead believers into thinking that obedience is legalism.

Of course, obedience to gain God's favor *is* legalism and is of no value. However, obedience as a by-product of love is not only accepted by God, it is something that will always be present in a true faith relationship with Him.

There is only one way that people show that they love and trust a noble leader and that is by obeying that leader no matter what the consequences may be. A child shows love and honor to a parent by obeying that parent. And we show our love for God, not by rebelling against Him, not by taking His name in vain, and not by claiming to be His child and living like a child of the devil, but by lovingly obeying Him. Certainly, we should show more love and loyalty to God than we show to an earthly leader, but often that is not the case!

Let's say that you are an employee and you work for a wonderful boss (I have had some tremendous bosses in my life). This boss cares about you, provides the best benefits that are available, and looks out for your welfare as he does for all of his employees. Would you reward this boss by stealing from his organization, talking about him behind his back, failing to give him an honest day's work, and generally being disloyal to him and to his organization? Not if you are a decent person. Not if you have the love of God in your heart! Nor will you live in rebellion against God if you love Him. Obedience to Him will be easy, not difficult— and it will not be legalism!

When I was seven years old, my sister, Mary, was killed in an automobile accident at the age of eighteen. I will remember every detail of that horrible night as long as I live. As a result, I may have been overly protective of my children, telling them whom they could ride with and what they could ride on and in. Motorcycles, for instance, were out! Our kids were not allowed to own a "murder cycle," as I called them or to ride with anyone else on one. As an incentive, I promised each of my children ten dollars every time they turned down a ride on a motorcycle. They didn't need to document the occasion; I took their word for it. Once, one of my kids came to me and said, "Dad, you owe me thirty dollars. I turned down three invitations to ride on a motorcycle."

"Three people invited you to ride on a motorcycle?" I asked.

"No. I turned down this guy once, and then he asked me two more times, and I turned him down each time!" she replied.

At first, I started to protest that since all this happened on one occasion and the requests were all within a short space of time that I only owed her ten dollars. But I thought better of arguing about it and peeled off thirty dollars and gave them to her.

Often, the kids would tell me about turning down an offer to ride on a motorcycle that had happened some time in the past, but they wouldn't accept payment for it. They said, "Dad, we didn't want to go against your wishes and make you feel bad. And besides, we know that you are thinking about what is best for us." Then I knew their responses were ones of love. Not long ago, one of my children confessed that he had accepted some motorcycle rides as a young person. All these years later, it made both of us feel bad. Obedience brings happiness; disobedience brings a lot of sorrow. My kids knew that I loved them so much that I would give my very life for them, and usually, they responded with the obedience of love. Three of the four now have children of their own, and they know what that means—as do you, if you are a parent.

Without question, the key verse in this section of John 13 is verse 34, which speaks about a "new" commandment. But I think that it is significant that it is preceded by these words of Jesus: " 'Little children, I shall be with you a little while longer. You will seek Me; and as I said to the Jews, "Where I am going, you cannot come," so now I say to you' " (verse 33).

Why did Jesus preface verse 34 with this statement? What is the significance?

I see two very important points here. First, Jesus, the only Example of true love the world has ever known, is about to leave this world. Jesus is Love personified, for He is God, and "God is love" (1 John 4:8). Without Jesus' presence, how is the world to know what true love is? The answer is that the world was to see this love in His disciples. Jesus was leaving, but now His disciples were to love as He loved.

Second, I see importance in the way the disciples were to transfer the love they felt for their Master to a love for one another. There's no question that the eleven disciples who were left after Judas's departure, loved Jesus. But, for the most part, they had shown anything but love for each other. The vertical love the disciples had for Jesus must now be expressed horizontally in their love for each other and for all other Christians.

So Jesus tells them that He has a "new" commandment. Some people look at Jesus' use of the term *new* commandment and get the idea that it replaces the "old" commandment, specifically the Ten Commandments. Nothing could be further from the truth. *New* can mean "in addition to what has come before." Or it can also mean a greater understanding of the previous commandment, an enhancement or magnification of it. For instance, Jesus said, "By no means will even a jot or a tittle of the law be changed" (see Matthew 5:18). He then amplified the law by showing that not only should we not kill but that even hatred is also a violation of this commandment. So if we truly love God and man, we will live in harmony with God's ten love requirements.

You may recall that when Jesus was asked what was the great commandment, He first quoted Deuteronomy 6:5, " 'Love the LORD your God with all your heart.' " This embodies the first four of the Ten Commandments. Then He added, " ' "You shall love your neighbor as yourself" ' " (Leviticus 19:18), which covers the last six.

Now, in John 13, Jesus tells His disciples, " 'A new commandment I give to you, that you love one another; as I have loved you' " (verse 34). This "new" commandment is not new in content, but it is new in scope. Leviticus 19:18 is speaking of your Jewish neighbor, your physical neighbor, or your family relationships. Jesus is speaking here in verse 34 of your spiritual family. This means that we are to love any believer in Jesus—regardless of race, national origin, economic status, educational level, and so on—as a brother or sister in Christ. And not only are we to love these brothers and sisters, Jesus says we are to love them, "As I have loved you."

That's a tall order. How does Jesus Christ love us? I think that the apostle Paul describes this kind of love very well in two places. First, in his "love chapter," 1 Corinthians 13, and again in Ephesians 4:32. To the Ephesians, Paul wrote,

"Be kind to one another, tenderhearted, forgiving one another, even as God in Christ forgave you."

So, first, we see that the love of Christ is kind. Christ demonstrated kindness to the woman taken in adultery. He even showed kindness to Judas, His betrayer. He created no scene when He confronted Judas. In fact, He was so calm that the other disciples thought He was sending Judas on an errand, which in a sense He was.

Paul's love chapter, 1 Corinthians 13, is the measure of love, the standard of love, that Jesus revealed so perfectly. And it begins with kindness. "Love suffers long and is kind; love does not envy; love does not parade itself, is not puffed up; does not behave rudely, does not seek its own, is not provoked, thinks no evil; does not rejoice in iniquity, but rejoices in the truth; bears all things, believes all things, hopes all things, endures all things" (1 Corinthians 13:4–7).

Now, because God is love and because Jesus is God, we can replace the word *love* with the name *Jesus.* Sometime, try reading 1 Corinthians 13 replacing the word *love* with *Jesus.* "Jesus suffers long and is kind; Jesus does not envy . . ." That's a beautiful description of Jesus, isn't it? But there is more. Jesus asks us to love as He loves. So, now put your name where the word *love* appears in 1 Corinthians 13 and read the chapter that way. For example, "Jim suffers long and is kind; Jim does not envy . . ." It's quite humbling, isn't it? I wish those words described me; don't you wish they described you? If we read the Word of God as applying to ourselves and not to someone else, it will always bring us to our knees. I had read the Beatitudes many times and thought they were beautiful, poetic words. Then I preached a series of sermons on them, and as I carefully studied each one, I was greatly convicted of my own spiritual need.

In Ephesians 4:32, the key word following "be kind" is *tenderhearted.* Of course, kindness is a result of a tender heart. When we love as Christ loved, we will be tenderhearted, sensitive to the needs of others. Christ loved His disciples selflessly, sacrificially, and understandingly. To do this, He had to be sensitive to their needs. He didn't think of what He wanted but of what they needed. Often we think first of what we want to receive or what we want to see happen. But if we love as Jesus loved, we won't put our happiness first; we'll think, not of ourselves, but of others. This was the tenderness that Jesus demonstrated and that led Him to truly understand His disciples.

Finally, Ephesians 4:32 says we are to be "forgiving [to] one another, even as God in Christ forgave you." There is no greater example of forgiveness than God's forgiving us. His Son, Jesus, understood that and immediately forgave those who crucified Him. He did not say, "I'll forgive them someday." He didn't say, "I'll forgive them if they ask Me to forgive them." Jesus taught that if someone sins against you seven times in one day and asks you to forgive him, you should do it (see Luke 17:3, 4). This is the most important part of loving as Jesus loved—asking for forgiveness from those we have harmed and granting forgiveness to those who have harmed us, either physically or emotionally.

I have walked into churches where you could feel the tension and lack of love radiating from the members. Often people will go to a church like that, and even though people speak to them, they feel that the church is unfriendly and they leave with that impression. Friendliness is not demonstrated by glad-handing the visitors. Visitors are quick to observe how the members treat each other. Nonverbal communication speaks louder than words. Visitors may not know one thing about differences between the members, particularly between church leaders, but they will still sense that something is wrong between the members of that church—something left over from the last board meeting, nominating committee, or some soured business deal between members.

On the other hand, when you fellowship with a church group that has harmony, you will see and feel the love between the members, and you will be drawn to them, because love for another one is catching. A number of years ago when I was pastoring the Arlington, Texas, congregation, we had a stewardship consultant, L. H. Coleman, conduct a church "capital stewardship" program. Part of this program was an all-church banquet held at a local hotel. One of the hotel's waiters at this banquet, a Muslim from a Middle Eastern country, was blown away by the love and unity he felt the church members had for each other and by the friendliness they showed to him. He said he had served many banquets but had never seen anything like this group. He got acquainted with Howard Conley, one of the leaders in our congregation, and told him, "I want to belong to a group like this." Of course, Howard was ready to share Jesus Christ with him, and he did.

We can't observe God's Ten Commandments without observing the most important commandment of all—the "new" commandment of love. If you don't love God and love one another, you have missed the essence of God's law. God is love, and God wants us to have His love in our hearts and demonstrate it to others! " 'By this all will know that you are My disciples, if you have love for one another' " (John 13:35).

Chapter 2 — John 14

"Let Not Your Heart Be Troubled"

The first memory verse I remember learning is John 3:16. The second is John 14:1–3 in the King James Version, which is still my favorite version for all the memory verses that I've learned. "Let not your heart be troubled: ye believe in God, believe also in me. In my Father's house are many mansions: if it were not so, I would have told you. I go to prepare a place for you. And if I go and prepare a place for you, I will come again, and receive you unto myself; that where I am, there ye may be also" (KJV). I've repeated that verse many times since learning it as a child. Many times I've started to recite it but haven't gotten past that first phrase, "Let not your heart be troubled." There is so much meaning in just those first few words.

When Christ spoke these words to His disciples, He knew they were getting ready to enter into a very turbulent time. The Jews were looking for the Messiah, but they had a whole different concept of the Promised One than they should have. They were looking for a military Messiah— one who would come and free them from the oppression of Rome. One who would restore them to prominence in the world, the national prominence they had had in the time of David and Solomon. They were looking for a Messiah who would set up a kingdom right then and right there that would last forever.

They knew the prophecies of Daniel, but they sadly misunderstood them. They knew about the image of Daniel 2; don't think for a minute that they didn't! They knew they were living in the time of the fourth kingdom—the kingdom of Rome—but they believed that the stone cut out without hands, was the kingdom that the Messiah would set up any day now, right there in Jerusalem. Even the disciples believed this was going to happen. Remember James and John and their request to be seated on the right and left of Jesus when He came into His kingdom?

When Jesus entered Jerusalem, riding on a donkey in what we now call the triumphant entry or Palm Sunday, the disciples thought, *He's actually going to do it!* Then, all of a sudden, Christ started telling them, "No, I'm not going to set up a worldly kingdom. I'm going away, but I'll return for you." They had all kinds of trouble with this. They had sat at His feet for three years, but they still hadn't realized what He was trying to teach them. They had miserably failed the test of humility as we saw in John 13. Now their world was about to fall apart. They were about to witness the death of their Master on the cross. And Jesus tried to prepare them for what lay ahead by saying to them, " 'Let not your heart be troubled' " (John 14:1).

That is still His message to us today. Sometimes He asks us to deliver that message to someone, and it's a difficult thing to do. It's hard to walk into the hospital room of a cancer patient and tell him, "Let not your heart be troubled." Or to say to a parent whose child is on drugs, "Let not your heart be troubled." Imagine how hard it is to stand with a man who is sobbing because his marriage has been destroyed and his wife and children are leaving him, and say to him, "Let not your heart be troubled." Or picture yourself saying to a broken and abused woman, "Let not your heart be troubled."

When *are* we to be troubled? Is there anything so terrible that it's finally all right to get stressed out about? Jesus didn't live in some kind of a Pollyanna dream world. He knew more about trouble than we will ever know. In fact, He was there when trouble got started—and He knew who and what caused it! But Jesus gave us a formula for getting through every difficulty. He told us how to not let our current situation or dilemma crush us.

Jesus went on to tell the disciples, " 'I will not leave you orphans' " (verse 18). To be an orphan is to be fatherless. "I will not leave you fatherless," Jesus told them, "even though I am going away, you will not be orphans. I will come to you." " 'A little while longer and the world will see Me no more, but you will see Me. Because I live, you will live also. At that day you will know that I am in My Father, and you in Me, and I in you' " (verses 19, 20). Jesus promised them the indwelling of His Holy Spirit. *I promise you that you won't be alone.*

Verse 21 says, " 'He who has My commandments and keeps them, it is he who loves Me. And he who loves Me will be loved by My Father, and I will love him and manifest Myself to him.' " In this day of focusing on righteousness by faith, we sometimes want to put obedience aside. But that's not a true understanding of righteousness by faith. The Bible says, "When I was a child, . . . I understood as a child" (1 Corinthians 13:11). When I first discovered righteousness by faith, I was so excited by the fact that Jesus had done it all for me, that my first response was, "I don't have to do anything!"

That's right. I *don't* have to do anything. But let me tell you something else. Through the indwelling of the Holy Spirit and through the love of the Lord Jesus Christ, we will see a change take place in our lives. It's true that we're not saved by what we do. In fact, the prophet Isaiah said that all our righteous acts are like filthy rags (see Isaiah 64:6). He didn't say that our sins are like filthy rags. We know our sins are bad and ugly. Instead, Isaiah says that our *righteous* actions are like filthy rags! That's how impossible it is for anything we do to count toward our salvation.

Even when we are trying to serve the Lord, we aren't responding perfectly. So our obedience isn't what saves us. But if we are trusting Jesus for our salvation, we will be obedient. Listen to what Christ said—the order in which He puts things. " '*If you love Me,* keep My commandments' " (John 14:15; emphasis added). Love is first, followed by obedience. Love has to be first. Love comes before anything else. Obedience can't be first. Obedience is the result of love. Jesus says that if we have a love relationship with Him, our lives are going to be changed. We're going to be in harmony with Him. He will live in us, and we will live in Him, and our lives will change. Love will bring about obedience. That's just the way a love relationship works.

Finally, He says, " 'And he who loves Me will be loved by My Father, and I will love him and manifest Myself to him' " (verse 21). So we see this order:

1. Love.
2. A trusting obedience in Jesus Christ and a trusting

relationship resulting from that love.

3. Ultimate safety by dwelling in Christ.

" 'You in Me,' " Jesus said, " 'and I in you' " (verse 20). And He goes on to say, " 'If anyone loves Me, he will keep My word; and My Father will love him, and We will come to him and make Our home with him' " (verse 23).

What is the formula? Love, trusting obedience, and ultimate safety by living in Jesus.

No wonder Jesus could tell the disciples, "Let not your heart be troubled." Troublesome times will come, but you don't have to have a troubled heart. We must face the fact that this world is going to self-destruct. We are going to lose the things of this world; therefore, we cannot depend on them. The sooner we face this, the sooner we'll have peace!

We are certainly not going to be able to depend on money. Our worldwide economic meltdown has reminded us of that! In time, we will lose every red cent. We might not lose our money right away, but we will lose it. One way or another it will be taken from us. It may be in the current economic fiasco, or it may be taken from us by a funeral, but, eventually, we will lose everything.

I used to say that I'd never seen a hearse pulling a U-Haul trailer, but then one day I did! I was driving down the freeway, and there came a hearse, pulling a U-Haul trailer! So I'll never be able to say that again. Some hippie had bought an old hearse and was pulling a U-Haul trailer with it!

But that hearse was not in a funeral procession. It is still true that we can't take it with us when we go. There will be an end to life as we know it. We will face one of two things:

the grave or the Second Coming.

Life isn't going to keep on just like it is today, so we need to prepare for that eventuality. And this preparation means we must quit putting off establishing a relationship with Jesus Christ. How often have we said, "Well, I'm going to build a relationship with Jesus Christ, one of these days"?

We must do it now, because now is really the only time we have!

Jesus Christ has given us this tremendous gift of salvation. He's given us true security in a world in which there is absolutely no other security! Jesus can say, "Let not your heart be troubled" because He knows your immediate problems. He knows all about the cancer or other terrible health problems you're facing. He knows all about the family problems that consume your thoughts. He knows whatever trial or stress or worry you're facing—and He will bring you through them and even guarantee your ultimate safety—if you have a relationship with Him.

It's a relationship of love, trust, and obedience. It's a relationship that trusts Him enough to say, "Lord, I know that what You're telling me in Your Word is exactly what is best for me. And because it's impossible for me to do this myself, I ask You to come into my life and change me by living in me. Please give me the kind of victorious life that You want for me!"

When you do this, you will begin to look at life in a different way. You will begin to realize that there is ultimate safety in Jesus Christ and that no matter what your circumstances may be, you can handle what life deals to you because you know that by trusting in Him and resting in Him, ultimately it will be all right. There's victory in our Lord and Savior, Jesus Christ, and this is His gift to us.

I often hear people say, "I love Him, but I don't need to obey Him. I don't need to keep His commandments; I just need to love Him."

That's not a response of love, is it? If a wife tells a husband, "I love you and I care for you," but she has other lovers, there is something very wrong about that love. The same is true if a man is telling his wife, "I love you," but every time she looks around, he's with another woman. That's not true love.

Jesus tells us that if we love Him, we're not going to continue running around with the devil. "For this is the love of God, that we keep His commandments" (1 John 5:3). Jesus says, "If you love Me, you're going to want to have a relationship with Me as your Lord, your Savior, and your God." Then He says, " 'You believe in God, believe also in Me' " (John 14:1).

It was very difficult for the disciples to believe in Jesus. At one point, Philip said, " 'Lord, show us the Father, and it is sufficient for us.' " Jesus replied, " 'Have I been with you so long, and yet you have not known Me, Philip? He who has seen Me has seen the Father' " (verses 8, 9). Jesus came to show us exactly what the Father is like. Jesus is God who came to this earth, grew up in an ordinary home, and was not ashamed to do common, everyday carpenter work.

He knew temptation too; far more temptation than we'll ever face! There's no question that the devil did everything he could to get Jesus to sin; he was smart enough to know that if he could bring the Master down, then he had us all! Satan would be victorious in his battle with Christ if he could tempt Him into sin even once.

In Jesus we see a loving God—a God who cares and a

God who is strong, not weak. In Jesus we see a God who is willing to die for us on the cross. As humans, our great temptation is to try to *act* like God, rather than *be* Godlike, which Jesus was. We try to elevate ourselves above those around us, acting like we're something we're not. Jesus says, "Believe in God and believe also in Me, because We're One and the same."

" 'In My Father's house are many mansions' " (verse 2). Now when I was a child and learned that verse, I wondered what it meant. *Inside of My Father's house there are a lot of mansions?* That didn't quite seem right. And if so, what did it mean?

Some of the newer Bible translations say, " 'In My Father's house are many rooms [many suites, many apartments].' " And that reminds me of the time I was waiting for a bus in London. The bus stop was right in front of an apartment house called Bromley Mansions or something like that. Suddenly, I realized what the old King James translation was saying! There is a room in the Father's house for everyone! There is a room for you, and there is a room for me. There is a room for everyone who wants to live in the Father's house. No one is ever turned away who sincerely wants to live with God. That's what Jesus meant.

I'll never forget the sermon about heaven that my college homiletics teacher once gave to our class. He told us we needed to make heaven real when we preached! Then he told us that he had a blueprint with the exact layout of how he wanted his mansion in heaven to be. Really. I'm not making this up. He was already planning the furnishings and the landscaping and the dimensions and locations of all the rooms. That's a little *too real* for me—drawing a blueprint of my mansion in heaven!

The important thing about heaven is that Jesus Christ is going to be there. Then, after a thousand years, He's going to come back to this earth, and the Holy City will come with Him! Jesus will bring us back with Him, and He will rebuild this earth. And best of all, He'll live with us forever! The important thing is not the place. Being with Jesus—that's what heaven is all about. It's not about missing out on a mansion. In fact, this concept of a room in our heavenly Father's house is more beautiful than having a mansion, don't you think? Just think about it. Living in God's house, having a room there. Going down sometimes to His big living room and spending time with the Creator of the universe! That's got to be more wonderful than living in a big, old lonely mansion! Just being with Jesus—and being reunited with our loved ones—that's what heaven is all about!

Then Jesus continues, " 'If it were not so, I would have told you' " (verse 2). Those are some of the most reassuring words in all of Scripture. I was in a Sabbath School class discussion years ago with a very intelligent man who was teaching on the subject of Creation. Amazingly, he doubted the Creation story, and that became very apparent when he made the statement, "But what did Moses know about how this world was created, anyway? He's the one who wrote Genesis, and what did he know about it?"

Now I usually don't talk much in Sabbath School classes. I usually sit back quietly, but I had to answer that question!

"I'll tell you what he knew about it," I answered. "Moses knew what God told him—and God was there at Creation. Furthermore, Jesus Christ was there, too, because the Bible says that it was through Jesus that all the worlds were created."

When I read Jesus' words, I'm so reassured, "If it were not so, I would have told you." Jesus Christ came to this earth, and John is telling us that Jesus is the Creator. Christ Himself is indicating that He is the Creator and that if it were not so, He would have told us. We don't have to worry about how this world came into existence. If it hadn't come into existence exactly as the Bible says it did, then Jesus would have told us! He would have set us straight.

I accept the creation of this earth by faith in Jesus Christ. No, I don't understand it, but I believe it 100 percent. Why? Because Jesus said, "If it were not so, I would have told you." The Bible tells us how it all began, and Jesus confirms it. And that settles it for me!

Then He says, " 'I go to prepare a place for you. And if I go and prepare a place for you, I will come again and receive you unto Myself; that where I am, there you may be also' " (verses 2, 3). What would we do if we really believed that? Would it change us? Would it change our lives? Would it change our emphases? Christ says that He's coming again. Do we really believe it? Are we telling the world? We have a duty to do so, particularly to those who want to hear it.

In Matthew 28:19, 20, Jesus gives us the gospel commission: " 'Go therefore and make disciples of all the nations, baptizing them in the name of the Father and of the Son and of the Holy Spirit, teaching them to observe all things that I have commanded you; and lo, I am with you always, even to the end of the age.' " We must never fail to get that message out, but we need to balance it. Some speak too much about it, and others not enough. It needs to be central in our talking, planning, and working long term—as if it might be a hundred years before His return. But we must live, preach, teach, and talk as if He were returning today or tomorrow.

As Adventists, we know so much about end-time prophecies that we're lulled to sleep. We sit back and say, "Well, you know, this hasn't happened yet," or, "That hasn't happened yet." "A national Sunday law hasn't been enacted yet, and as a matter-of-fact, it seems like it's being pushed a little further away. So we don't really have anything to worry about."

Has it ever dawned on you that when God says He'll cut time short, that He might cut out something we think must happen before He comes? He's God, you know, and He can do exactly what He pleases. What if He decides, "I'm going to cut that out. The chart's over; I'm not going to finish the rest of that"?

If you look at God's record, you'll see that there have been times He did that very thing. The Jews missed the whole idea of the Messiah and His kingdom because they thought He was going to follow their chart. He didn't.

What if God were to say, "That's enough! I'm going back to get my children"? He couldn't say that too soon for most of us! I want Him to come so badly, and I want Him to come soon. But I wonder if there isn't someone else I need to tell about His love before that happens? I wonder if there isn't someone else He wants you to share His love with before He comes back? Why don't you pray for Him to lead you to somebody whom you can lead to Him? Pray that He will open up a conversation for you with somebody. And pray that instead of turning, walking away, and ignoring that conversation, you'll realize it is an opportunity given you by the Lord to quietly and lovingly lead that person to Jesus.

There's something even better than going to heaven—it's taking someone with you!

" 'If I go and prepare a place for you, I will come again and receive you to Myself; that where I am, there you may be also' " (John 14:3).

During World War II, a soldier who had been badly injured came home. He had lost his right arm and a portion of his face. His wounds were so bad that he was totally disfigured. His family was glad to have him back home, but they felt uncomfortable in his presence. Try as they might, they just couldn't stay in his room very long before they excused themselves to go somewhere else. The young soldier began to realize that they were avoiding him and that when they were in the same room with him, they seemed very sad. So he called his family together and said, "Listen, I can tell that you really don't want to be with me."

"It isn't that we don't want to be with you," they replied. "But when we see you like this, we remember how alive you once were and how handsome. It just saddens us so much to see you like this. We're just having a hard time handling it."

He said, "I don't want you to have a hard time with this. Let me tell you what happened when I got hurt. I was lying there on the battlefield injured badly. I was slipping in and out of consciousness, and I was praying. Then I had a dream in which I saw a form coming across the battlefield. Hand grenades were going off, and there was gunfire all about Him, but the explosions never touched Him. Then, as He leaned over me, He said, 'I am the Good Shepherd, and I love you. I want you to believe in Me, and I want to offer you eternal life.' In my dream, my vision, or whatever it was, I said to Him, 'I accept You as my Savior.' And then I felt such a deep peace in my heart—even there on the battlefield. And that peace is still in my heart right now, so that it doesn't even matter to me that I've lost an arm. It doesn't even matter to me that I'm disfigured and crippled. I have the assurance that Jesus is preparing a place for me and that He's coming back for me one of these days."

He continued, "Folks, will you relax when you are with me? Because I want you to know that I'm seeing beyond today. I'm seeing that ultimate safety Jesus has for me—that home that He's preparing for me."

Can you see beyond the troubles of today? Can you see past the trials and the heartaches and the problems you face—severe though they may be? Can you trust in Jesus? When He says, "Let not your heart be troubled," can you relax and give it all over to Him and let His peace flood your soul? Are you looking forward to living in His house and spending time with Him throughout eternity? There's a room in His house for you! If it weren't so, He would have told us.

So, let not your heart be troubled!

Chapter 3 — John 15

CHRIST'S LAST WILL

My two sons and I have made a few trips together—just the three of us. The first trip was to Washington, D.C. We had a great time; we really did. Now, we always had fun on family vacations with the whole family too. But, you know, there is something very, very special about spending time with just your children. Of course, that means not just sons but daughters too. There is a special bond between me and my daughters; I couldn't be closer to anyone than I am to them. My daughters have a great sense of humor and love to have a good time. And I have a great time whenever I get to be with them. But on this particular trip to Washington, D.C., my sons came along with me. We saw the sights in Washington, and then we went up to New York City where I had some business to take care of. From New York, we went on to Boston where we watched a baseball game at Fenway Park. There are very few places in America like Fenway Park in Boston and Wrigley Field in Chicago to make you feel like you have gone back fifty or sixty years in time. These are antique ballparks, built long before most of us were born. My sons and I just had a great time together on that trip.

Several summers later, they said, "Dad, we've got to do a trip together again." Jimmy was getting serious about a girl, and we all knew it wouldn't be long before he would be married and it would be a different situation then. So the boys said, "We've got to do another trip."

"Well, I'm going to California," I told them, "and I'll take you with me." And I did.

In the morning, I would do my work, and my sons would hang around the motel, resting, catching up on their reading, watching a little television, or swimming. Then I would come roaring in about two or three o'clock and say, "Let's go do something!" And we'd start off.

One day they said, "Dad, let's go to Disneyland—just for two or three hours." (Actually, this was on our last day in California, on our way to the airport!) "We went to Disneyland as kids," they said, "and we'd like to go back."

"OK." I replied, "That will be great!"

So we went. We got to Disneyland, and the boys were going here and there and riding things. I was just kind of wandering around. I would go with them to a ride or an attraction and then just wait for them outside. Finally, they said, "Dad, come on! Go on this ride with us!"

Now, I'll tell you a little secret. Amusement park rides and I don't get along very well anymore. As a kid, I loved roller coasters. I really did. But today there are some of these rides with all this motion that can really get me out of whack. I've got a little inner-ear problem or something that gets out of balance. I remember as a teenager riding something called The Hammer at the Texas state fair. Do you remember that old ride? It had two compartments on each end of a long arm; you went around and around, twisting and turning and all that sort of thing. I remember getting on it, and I remember getting off with all my equilibrium gone and walking to the middle of the midway where I lost all the stuff I had just eaten! And then trying to remain "cool" in front of my friends. That's hard to do! So when the boys began urging me to ride with them at Disneyland, all those memories came back. I knew Jimmy liked all of the rides, the wilder the better! From the time he was a little kid, I'd take him to the fair and try to keep him away from the rides. But, no, we had to go down to the midway, and small as he was, he'd get on the fastest, wildest rides. He would get this look of glee in his eyes, you know. *How can this kid take this?* I wondered. *This contraption is jerking him all over the place. His hair is blowing every direction; and he's got this beautiful look of ecstasy on his face.*

So at Disneyland that day, the boys said, "Dad, there's a ride here called Space Mountain. It's kind of like a space ride, you know. Come on and go with us."

Against my better judgment, I joined them in the longest line I have ever been in throughout my entire life. I've never stood in line for anything that long. We visited and talked, and, finally, all of a sudden, we were at the head of the line! Now when I heard the words *Space Mountain,* I was imagining something like the time I went to an observatory. I thought Space Mountain must be some easy sort of educational ride where it was quiet and smooth, like being out in space and you could look at the stars. *It will be neat,* I thought.

All in the world it was, however, was a roller coaster in a building! That's it. A roller coaster in the dark! Now I can handle a roller coaster—if I can see where I'm going. But a roller coaster in the dark with lots of flashing lights and other things that can make you dizzy, that is something else altogether. My boys were in the two seats right in front of me, and I was in the next seat all by myself. I couldn't see my knuckles, but I knew they were white, because I was really holding on! My boys were waving their hands in the air and shouting and having the best time in the world, while I was praying, "Lord, just let me live through this. Let me live long enough to get off this thing. Help me not to get sick! I promise You I will never ride this again!"

Somehow, the Lord answered my prayer. I staggered off. The boys jumped out and shouted, "That was great! Let's go again!" I was barely able to stand upright; the whole world spun around me. The boys looked at me and asked, "Dad, are you all right?"

"I've lost my equilibrium," I told them. I guess I sounded quite scientific or something. I wish I had just said, "I'm dizzy" or something like that. They burst into laughter. They couldn't contain themselves. Even today, as a family joke, they ask me, "Have you lost your equilibrium today?"

So they took me by the arm, one on each side, and led me to a place where I could sit down. I was definitely not feeling all that well, but I'm going to tell you the truth—down inside, I was happy! It's crazy. I was going through something that was so miserable, yet deep down inside, I was honestly thinking, *this is probably a moment my sons will cherish and will always recall with laughter.* I had a joy and a peace even in that awful situation. I still do, just thinking about it.

It took me a while to recover. In fact, I had to lie down in the back seat of the car and let them drive. We went to the airport, where we were bumped off our flight, so we spent another night there. Then we continued our little vacation together.

But, you know, joy is something that exceeds happiness. Joy is something that is so deep that it is much greater than happiness. Happiness is dependent upon externals. Happiness is dependent upon the weather. Happiness is dependent upon all the conditions around you being just exactly the way you want. Happiness is dependent on staying off of roller coasters that run around inside a dark building! But joy is deeper—far deeper. We don't really understand and use the word *joy* like we should. I think if we had a phrase in our church that we should use and remember, it should be something like *Don't miss the joy of being a Christian!* Don't miss it. The joy of being in Jesus is so important. And that is what Jesus was talking about in John 15:11, " 'These things I have spoken to you, that My joy may remain in you, and that your joy may be full.' "

Jesus doesn't use words that don't have depth of meaning. So when He talks about joy and full joy, He's talking about something important and significant. He's talking about the spiritual joy that He offers each of us. He said, "I want you to have that kind of joy."

A gloomy Christian is a contradiction of terms, and nothing has done Christianity more harm than its connection with dark clothes and long faces. Why do so many people have the idea that when you become a Christian, you have to give up all the joy in life? Why do people, especially young people, feel that they can't enjoy life and be Christians? At least in part, it's because we Christians have done such a poor job of receiving, demonstrating, and living that full joy that Jesus says He wants us to have. When people see this solemn, serious, grim attitude that we present as spirituality, it turns them away. They look at that, and they say, "Who needs it!" Jesus said, "I want your joy to be full. I want it to be complete." And He gave us a prescription of exactly how to have that kind of joy.

Let's get the setting. You remember that John tells us how Jesus and His disciples ate the Passover meal in the upper room—the last time they would all be together like that with their Master (see John 13). Then Jesus began to give the disciples some final counsel—His last will, if you please. These words are Christ's final legacy that He gave to the disciples the last night He was to be with them before His arrest, trial, and crucifixion. So these are significant, important words—Christ's last will.

You know, it's amazing how seriously we take ourselves. We take ourselves too seriously, and yet we don't take God's promises seriously enough. Jesus began His final words to the disciples by saying,

> "I am the true vine, and my Father is the gardener. He cuts off every branch in me that bears no fruit, while every branch that does bear fruit he prunes so that it will be even more fruitful. You are already clean because of the word I have spoken to you. Remain in me, and I will remain in you. No branch can bear fruit by itself; it must remain in the vine. Neither can you bear fruit unless you remain in me.
>
> "I am the vine; you are the branches. If a man remains in me and I in him, he will bear much fruit; apart from me you can do nothing. If anyone does not remain in me, he is like a branch that is thrown

away and withers; such branches are picked up, thrown into the fire and burned. If you remain in me and my words remain in you, ask whatever you wish, and it will be given you. This is to my Father's glory, that you bear much fruit, showing yourselves to be my disciples.

"As the Father has loved me, so have I loved you. Now remain in my love. If you obey my commands, you will remain in my love, just as I have obeyed my Father's commands and remain in his love. I have told you this so that my joy may be in you and that your joy may be complete" (John 15:1–11, NIV).

Now Israel regarded itself as the vine. The vine was the national symbol, like the eagle is the symbol of the United States. The Israelites said, "We are the vine." That's what they were saying as a nation. In fact, they took this symbol from the Old Testament where God spoke of Israel as a vine:

I will sing for the one I love
    a song about his vineyard;
My loved one had a vineyard
    on a fertile hillside.
He dug it up and cleared it of stones
    and planted it with the choicest vines.
He built a watchtower in it
    and cut out a winepress as well.
Then he looked for a crop of good grapes,
    but it yielded only bad fruit.
"Now you dwellers in Jerusalem and men of Judah,
    judge between me and my vineyard.

What more could have been done for my vineyard
    than I have done for it?
When I looked for good grapes,
    why did it yield only bad?
Now I will tell you
    what I am going to do to my vineyard:
I will take away its hedge,
    and it will be destroyed;
I will break down its wall,
    and it will be trampled.
I will make it a wasteland,
    neither pruned nor cultivated,
    and briers and thorns will grow there.
I will command the clouds
    not to rain on it."

The vineyard of the LORD Almighty
    is the house of Israel,
and the men of Judah
    are the garden of his delight.
And he looked for justice, but saw bloodshed;
    for righteousness, but heard cries of distress
      (Isaiah 5:1–7, NIV).

So Israel regarded itself as the vine of Judah. In fact, at the entrance of the temple itself, was a carving of a beautiful vine inlaid with gold and grapes growing on it. Israel thought of itself as the vine. Then Jesus came along and said, " 'I am the true vine' " (John 15:1). This is one of His "I am" statements in the book of John. There are several of them. He says, " 'I am the way, the truth, and the life' " (John 14:6). " 'I am the bread of life' " (John 6:48). " 'I am

the light of the world' " (John 8:12). " 'I am the good shepherd' " (John 10:11). And now He says to the disciples, "I
am the true vine."

The disciples knew exactly what Jesus meant. They understood that He was telling them, "Don't look any longer
to Israel and your heritage for your salvation, to the fact
that you were born a Jew. I'm the Vine; you now must look
to Me for salvation. And this living, vital, saving relationship with Me comes from a connection—a fellowship of
love—that is as close and essential as the life-giving connection of the branch to the vine." That's the secret of the relationship—staying connected to the Vine. That's where all
the fruit comes from in your life. You're not obedient so
that you can be God's child. You're obedient, *because you
are already God's child.* And because His life-giving power
goes out from the vine into the branches like sap, you bring
forth fruit as a result of that divine connection. You cannot
have the fruit that Christ wants you to have without that
vital connection. You cannot do it. Any fruit that is pro-
duced apart from that connection with Him is only wild
grapes.

When Camille and I were first married and were at An-
drews University, we lived in an apartment out on a high-
way for a while. This apartment had been old chicken coop.
The owner had cleaned the chickens out and made it into
an apartment, and really, it wasn't too bad. Nobody else
would rent it because they had seen it when it was a chicken
coop and knew what it had been. We had never seen it as a
chicken coop, so we thought it was a pretty nice place and
rented it. Later, people would tell us, "Oh yeah, we used to
see the chickens in this place." But we enjoyed living there.
It was right next to an orchard. The man that owned the

orchard told us we could go in there and pick an apple and eat it anytime we wanted to. "But," he said, "you have to eat whatever you pick right there; don't carry off any apples."

I used to look at those apples. You know, you don't eat a whole lot of apples when you're standing out in the middle of an orchard on a cold fall day. But I used to look at those apples, and I would think, *Those are beautiful apples. If I could just take a limb from one of those trees, break it off, and put it in the window, I could grow beautiful apples right in the apartment.* Of course, that is facetious; even I knew that. But it's no more silly than thinking that we can bring forth good works in our lives without a vital connection to Jesus Christ. A life-giving connection to the Vine is the only way that we can produce any kind fruit, the fruit of the Spirit, in our lives.

The apostle Paul tells us what the fruit of the Spirit is. "The fruit of the Spirit is love, joy, peace, longsuffering, kindness, goodness, faithfulness, gentleness, self-control" (Galatians 5:22, 23). Love is the first fruit of the Spirit, because God is love. The second is joy. Not just a joy that is stuck in our lives haphazardly. The joy that is a fruit of the Spirit is an inner joy that is present even when you are going through the most excruciating experiences of life. Even then, that joy is there. Why? Because of a living connection with Jesus Christ. Jesus says that if you will maintain that connection with Him, joy will remain in your heart and life—full joy, complete joy—even though you are going through the darkest days of your life. Your joy will be there even in adversity. It will be there because you are connected to Jesus Christ as the branch is connected to the vine.

Connection. That's the message of Christ's last will, His

legacy to the disciples and to us, in John 15. We could come at it from a hundred different directions, and we would still find the same thing. "Connect with Me," Jesus says, "and I will give you life. And that life will produce fruit." What, then, is our job? Our job is to maintain the connection. Our job is to understand that sometimes pruning must take place. Now, pruning is not the devastating trampling of the enemy coming into the vineyard and slashing and hacking away. That's not what Jesus is talking about. Pruning is carefully dealing with things in our lives that interfere with the connection.

There are some things that may need to be pruned from my life. Jesus may say, "Jim, you're not handling money all that well. I'm going to prune that away. You're not handling this or that very well. So I'm going to prune this or that away." And He begins to carefully cut those things out of my life. That kind of pruning helps us if we react positively to it. You see, when Jesus begins to prune something out of my life, I can react either one way or the other. I can react bitterly, and the pruning will destroy me. Or I can react positively by trusting Him, and I will see growth take place in my life. After the pruning takes place, I will see the beautiful foliage that comes forth, the fruit that comes as a result. Recently, I was in a place where they grow a lot of grapes. At the proper season, they prune the vines drastically— right down to the ground. Later, in the fall, there will be beautiful foliage as a result. The connection is so important. Holding on to Him, trusting Him, reading His words and making them a part of your life, trusting Him even in a time of adversity: these are the things that keep us fastened securely to the Vine.

A number of years ago, I was driving along the road when

my phone rang. My wife was calling to say that a friend's wife had died. She had just gotten the word, and actually, the funeral was taking place that very day. I quickly drove to the house, packed a few things, and rushed to the airport. I landed in the city where my friend lived and took a taxi to his home. I knew it was too late to make it to the funeral. When I got to the house, the family wasn't back from the cemetery yet. I hadn't been able to be at the funeral, but I knew that often it is when the funeral is over that you need a friend the most. I was sitting on the front step of the house when the family got back from the funeral. My friend was there with his sons and some close relatives—that's all. He greeted me, and he thanked me for coming. And for the next three days, he wouldn't let me leave his side. When it came time to go to bed, he said, "Please, don't leave me." So I made a pallet on the floor by the side of his bed, and I slept there for three nights as he grieved. His wife's death left so many questions, and he was hurting so desperately.

Finally, I had to go home. Since then, we never really ever talked much about that time. We never discussed it, though we had seen each other many times, and he had remarried and was very happy with the new wife that the Lord had sent him. But some years later, I was to speak briefly at a meeting of some fifty or sixty pastors. This friend introduced me when it was time for me to speak. And as he did so, he told the group about that experience. He said, "This man was the only friend who came to be with me out of all of my friends. He came and went through the toughest time in my life with me."

That night I had dinner with another man, a pastor who was attending the meeting. As we were visiting, he brought up what my friend had said in introducing me. Then he said, "Just the year before last, your friend knocked on my door at six o'clock in the morning to tell me that my son had died in an accident. Then he stayed with me and saw me through that terrible time."

That is how God shares His joy through each of us in difficult times. I'd seen my friend go through his time of grief and sorrow, and I'd seen him receive spiritual and emotional healing. I'd seen him restored to do God's work. And now, as I looked into the face of my dinner partner, I realized that he, too, had come through his tragedy by the grace of God. God had restored him. Yes, a great tragedy had come into his life. There was no way to get around that. He had suffered and experienced tremendous pain, grief, and sorrow—as have some of you. But he had come through it trusting God, and he still had the joy Christ promised. The joy was still there—the joy of Jesus—the joy that is there even when the whole world seems to fall in. The joy that comes, even through the tears, because you trust in Jesus and Him alone and you know that He will see you through.

" 'These things I have spoken to you,' " Jesus said, " 'that My joy may remain in you, and that your joy may be full' " (John 15:11).

"I Have Overcome the World"

It's not easy to be a Christian. It isn't today, and it certainly wasn't back in the time of the disciples. Here in John 16, Jesus is talking to His disciples following the Passover meal in the upper room. It's that short period of time between their last meal together and His crucifixion, so He wants to pack as much instruction and encouragement and counsel as He can into this crucial time. He warns them:

> "These things I have spoken to you, that you should not be made to stumble. They will put you out of the synagogues; yes, the time is coming that whoever kills you will think that he offers God service. And these things they will do to you because they have not known the Father nor Me. But these things I have told you, that when the time comes, you may remember that I told you of them" (John 16:1–4).

"I want you to know ahead of time," He says, "that it isn't going to be easy to follow Me. I don't want you to stumble when persecution and trouble come. They're going to put you out of the synagogue; they're even going to kill you." And, of course, that is exactly what happened in the early church.

It still isn't easy being a Christian today. They may not be putting you out of the church; they may not be trying to kill you, but even so, being a Christian takes determination, courage, and stamina. Being a true believer and follower of Jesus has never been for the weak and faint of heart.

Now, I know there are some people who intentionally try to bring persecution upon themselves. And there are some people who seem to attract trouble no matter what. That is just how they are; they draw trouble to themselves. So, it doesn't mean that you're following the truth of Jesus just because you are experiencing trouble. Maybe you've simply become obnoxious and difficult to get along with, and you really aren't all that spiritual. I've seen people cause problems that never needed to arise. That isn't what Jesus is talking about. He's talking about the fact that the world does not understand or accept true believers. He says, " 'These things they will do to you because they have not known the Father nor Me' " (verse 3).

Sometimes we think that once we become Christians and give our lives to Jesus, everything is going to be just smooth sailing from then on. Let me assure you that it's not going to be that way. Instead, many times life becomes more difficult when we accept Jesus and begin to live for Him. Can you think of a reason why that might be so? Wouldn't you imagine that the devil would redouble his temptations when he sees he is losing you? The devil is going to make sure that you have a difficult time of it once you decide to follow Jesus.

Sometimes when tough times come and things get really rough, we begin to think, *God's turned His back on me. Things aren't working out for me at all. God must not care about me.* But the truth is that God may be closer to you at that very moment than at any other time. Remember that! The disciples were feeling downhearted because Jesus kept talking about going away and giving up His life. They didn't understand Him; they were worried and apprehensive about the future. But Jesus was closer to them right then than at any time in His ministry. He said, " 'I tell you the truth. It is to your advantage that I go away; for if I do not go away, the Helper will not come to you; but if I depart, I will send Him to you' " (verse 7). The Holy Spirit is to be with us and in us, always. " 'I will pray the Father,' " Jesus told them, " 'and He will give you another Helper, that He may abide with you forever . . . He dwells with you and will be in you' " (John 14:16, 17).

But we don't always understand the work of the Holy Spirit. Sometimes we think, *If I have the Holy Spirit, everything is going to be working out for me.* But that isn't what Jesus said. He said that when the Spirit comes, He is going to convict you of sin and of righteousness and of judgment (see John 16:8). Now, when you receive Jesus and are baptized, you receive the Holy Spirit. The Holy Spirit actually comes upon you and lives in you. What does this mean? It means that every time you start to do something you should not do, the Holy Spirit is going to convict you of sin and tell you that you shouldn't do that thing. You may think it is your conscience speaking to you, but it isn't your conscience. It's the Spirit of God. The Holy Spirit is working in your life and saying to you, "No! Don't do that. Don't go that direction."

The closer we come to Jesus Christ, the closer and more filled we are with the Spirit of God, the less righteous we will feel. Ellen White tells us that the more we become like Jesus—the more we are filled with the Holy Spirit—the more we will realize and feel our unworthiness. The more we will see our sinfulness in all its depths:

> The nearer we come to Jesus, and the more clearly we discern the purity of his character, the more clearly shall we see the exceeding sinfulness of sin, and the less shall we feel like exalting ourselves. Those whom Heaven recognizes as holy ones are the last to parade their own goodness. Men who have lived near to God, men who would sacrifice life itself rather than knowingly commit a wrong act, men whom God has honored with divine light and power, have confessed the sinfulness of their own nature. They have put no confidence in the flesh, have claimed no righteousness of their own, but have trusted wholly in the righteousness of Christ. So will it be with all who behold the Saviour.[1]

When we really grasp and understand how much sin permeates our lives, we will realize that our only hope is the blood of Jesus. There is no other hope. Have you noticed that sometimes when you're talking with those who believe in perfection—that we can gain the victory over every sin and live perfect, sinless lives like Jesus did—that it becomes clear that they don't really understand what sin is? Even our motives for doing right can be wrong! Sin, you see, is not just

---

1. Ellen G. White, "The Danger of Self-confidence," *The Youth's Instructor,* June 5, 1902.

doing wrong things. Sin is also failing to do good things. It's not responding the way God would have us respond. Sin is a part of our nature. It's us! We are fallen, sinful human beings.

So as the Holy Spirit comes into our lives, He will convict us of even more sin than we were aware of before He entered. When Jesus said that the Holy Spirit would convict the world of sin, He didn't mean the Spirit would convict only unbelievers. No. He meant believers as well—you and me. The work of the Holy Spirit is to come into the lives of believers and convict us of sin. And He does that by shining the light of God's truth more and more into the dark places in our lives. He does that so we can confess those sins and let Jesus take care of them.

I believe that as a church, we're often afraid to really discuss the work of the Holy Spirit and to try to understand it. We are afraid to see the power of God in our lives. We're afraid it's going to lead us off into some kind of fanaticism, because we have seen some who have been led in that direction. We are afraid that we are going to overemphasize certain aspects of the Spirit's work, because we have seen that happen; we have seen those that have gone off on tangents concerning spiritual gifts and speaking in tongues, and we're afraid of that. You know, it's not a bad thing to be cautious. We need to be cautious. But I believe we can be too cautious. We can be so cautious that we're afraid even to invite the Holy Spirit into our lives. We can be so cautious that we're afraid to study the work of the Spirit and to try to understand His role in our lives. That's too cautious; that's going to the other extreme. We need the power of the Holy Spirit in our lives. I need it in my life; you need it in your life. As a Christian, living day to day, I need the power of the Holy Spirit.

It is amazing what we try to do in life without the power of God, without His Spirit. We start off down that road, and we trudge along, relying on ourselves and our own efforts to live a Christian life. Let me tell you, that's a difficult journey—actually, it's an impossible journey. We're all alone, unless we have the Spirit of God working in us.

Someone gave me a book a while back. It was written back in the 1800s by Dwight L. Moody, the famous nineteenth-century evangelist. Moody was a hard worker; he nearly ruined his health working for the Lord. Then he began to realize what the real need in his life was. As I read his book and the quotations from other preachers and writers that he included, I also did a little reading between the lines. I thought I began to see where Moody was getting his ideas. He was getting them from Charles Spurgeon, the great British preacher and pastor of the Metropolitan Tabernacle in London. You see, Moody used to go to England quite often. He would go to the Metropolitan Tabernacle and take a seat right on the front row of the balcony and lean over the rail and listen to Spurgeon preach. Moody was a famous evangelist, but he had never been ordained by man to be a minister. He was a shoe salesman when he became a Christian. He started out as a Sunday School teacher in a little church in Chicago and continued to work with those kids as his ministry. As his ministry continued and grew, he grew along with it until he was in full-time evangelism. But he found that he was working himself to death. He was traveling all over the United States, holding huge evangelistic meetings. He was having tremendous results, but it seemed that the burden was growing heavier and heavier. You see, he was trying to travel down that road largely in his own strength. He was traveling alone. Oh, the Lord was working with him and in him, but he was still trying to carry much of the load himself.

Then, Moody said, he found the secret of true spiritual power. I thought this statement in his book was very interesting. He said that the problem with preachers is not that they are working themselves into utter exhaustion. The problem is that they are working without the Spirit of God—and that's what is so exhausting to them. He said that if preachers were to work in the power of the Holy Spirit, they would have such joy and see such fruitage and so many evidences of God's leading in their work that they would never wear out and never get into trouble. And that's true. It's true, not only for preachers, it's true for every Christian believer.

I tell you, we need the power of the Spirit of God. I need it, and you need it. We all need it. "Yes," Jesus said, "you're going to have persecution and trouble in the Christian life. It isn't going to be easy. It may even come to the point that people will try to kill you for your faith. But you aren't going to have to travel alone along the road of the Christian life. I'm going to ask the Father to send the Holy Spirit to travel the road with you. He is going to be with you and in you. He's going to go with you throughout the journey— all the way. He's never going to leave you."

Those are comforting words. No matter what comes to us in life, the Holy Spirit will abide with us forever. But we have to hunger and thirst for His presence in our lives. It's like righteousness—we have to hunger and thirst for it. You have to want it more than you want a new home, more than you want a new car, more than you want a good-paying job, and more than you want to make money. You have to hunger and thirst for the presence of the Holy Spirit in your life just like you want food and drink when you're really hungry and thirsty. Have you ever missed a meal or two? Have you ever gone a day or so without eating? If so, you know what happens. It isn't long before all you can think about is food. Your stomach keeps telling you that you haven't sent anything down that way in a long time. Everything reminds you of something to eat. Well, that's how we need to feel about the Holy Spirit being in our lives. We need to want Him, hunger and thirst for Him. We have to want Him if we're going to have Him.

Jesus said, " 'When He, the Spirit of truth, has come, He will guide you into all truth; for He will not speak on His own authority, but whatever He hears He will speak; and He will tell you things to come. He will glorify Me, for He will take of what is Mine and declare it to you' " (John 16:13, 14). When the Spirit of God comes upon us, we glorify Jesus. We uplift Jesus. We will point the world to Jesus Christ and to His cross. By our words and by our lives, we will point men and women to the Cross and show them what Jesus did there. We'll tell them how His blood covers our sins and how He is the only One who can offer us forgiveness and eternal life.

Jesus doesn't say it will be easy. Even with the Holy Spirit in our lives, we're going to be facing trials, difficulties, and painful experiences. But He says that the pain will turn into joy—like when a woman gives birth to a child:

> "You will be sorrowful, but your sorrow will be turned into joy. A woman, when she is in labor, has sorrow because her hour has come; but as soon as she has given birth to the child, she no longer remembers the anguish, for the joy that a human be-

ing has been born into the world. Therefore you now have sorrow; but I will see you again and your heart will rejoice, and your joy no one will take from you" (verses 20–22).

Now, you ladies know what Jesus is talking about! The rest of us know mentally from having observed it, but we can't understand it like you can. I remember when Camille was expecting Maryann. Wow, was she ready for that baby to be born! Her mother came to visit us, and she gave Camille some kind of concoction to drink—orange juice mixed with castor oil or something like that. It was supposed to hurry up the birth. It didn't work, but Camille was ready to do almost anything to have that baby be born! You know, I've never heard a woman say, "I don't care anything about children, but I sure do enjoy having them; I just like experiencing the birth process." It's usually the other way around. Women don't enjoy the birth experience, but once the child is born, they sure do love them! When those little new infants are placed in their arms, they forget all about the morning sickness and the problems they've had for nine months and the pain of giving birth. Their pain is turned into joy. And that is what happens in our spiritual life as well. It's not easy following Jesus. There will be pain, sorrow, temptations, and trials. But there is joy in the Christian life as well. And that joy is found in our relationship with Jesus Christ and in the presence of the Holy Spirit in our lives. So there is joy now, today, as we follow Jesus. There is a peace and a joy that comes from serving Him. Yes, there is pain and sorrow, but there is joy and peace as well. And then, someday Jesus will come and all the troubles and sorrows of this world really will be swallowed up in eternal joy and happiness.

Some people think that is what Jesus was talking about—His second coming—when He told the disciples, " 'A little while, and you will not see Me; and again a little while, and you will see Me' " (verse 16). Some people read this verse and think Jesus was talking about His second coming. I don't think that is what He was talking about at all. When Jesus said a "little while," I think He meant a long while. He knew the Second Coming was not going to take place in a little while. In Matthew 24, Jesus told the disciples all the things that would have to happen in the world before He would actually return. It was going to take more than a "little while."

So what does He mean here? He goes on to tell the disciples, " 'Therefore you now have sorrow; but I will see you again and your heart will rejoice' " (verse 22). Jesus could be talking about one of two things. He could have meant, "I'm going to be with you only a little while longer—only a few more hours." The Crucifixion and the tomb were approaching quickly. Then in a "little while" (a few days) He came right back to them, appearing to them in the upper room after His resurrection. That could be what Jesus meant, and I think that *is* what He meant.

But He also could have been saying, "I'm with you only a little while longer, and then the Holy Spirit will come, and I will be with you again, living in your heart through Him." That could be what He meant. Either way, what Jesus was saying was very, very true. This is really what it was all about for the disciples—a love relationship with the Master. And that's what it's all about for us as well. It's all about a relationship of love with the One who loved us so much that He was willing to go to the cross and give His life for us. It's all about wanting to be a child of God, an adopted son or daughter of the heavenly Father, a "brother" or "sister" of Jesus, filled with the Holy Spirit. My friend, that's why we have to hunger and thirst for the Holy Spirit in our lives, not because we want spiritual power or gifts or position, but because we want that relationship of love with the Father, Son, and Holy Spirit. Love is what it's all about. " 'The Father Himself loves you,' " Jesus said, " 'because you have loved Me, and have believed that I came forth from God' " (verse 27).

I had a friend who used to talk about heaven and preach about heaven. He would say, "I already have my mansion all figured out. I have a drawing in my mind of how my home there is going to be laid out." Bless his heart, a mansion in heaven is not what it's all about! It's about Jesus—that's what it's all about. It's about a love relationship with Him. Instead of a mental blueprint of your heavenly mansion, why not have a mental list (or a written list) of all the things you want to talk about with Jesus? Actually, I'll probably just be absolutely tongue-tied when I see Him and won't be able to say anything. I'll need a thousand years or so to loosen up my tongue to the point that I will be able to ask Him a question. But we'll have eternity, and there has to be some time in eternity when I'll get to be with Him—just me and Him alone—and talk. You'll surely have your time as well. That's what it's all about—sonship, daughtership, Jesus, the Father, and love.

When I was a boy, we were poor. I didn't realize it, but we were. I know many of you were the same. My father had a little awning company; he would go out and put awnings on people's houses. I often went with him in his pickup truck. It had a rack on the back where he carried his ladders and other equipment. I remember being with Dad one day when I was about seven or eight years old. We stopped at a service station to get gas, and there was a man there who owned one of the big automobile dealerships in town. I knew who he was. He was well known in town because of the auto dealership, but also because he owned some big speedboats and went all over that part of the country racing them. It was a hobby. He was a very wealthy man with a large, fabulous home. He came over to my dad and said, "John . . ." (He called my dad "John"; most people called him "Red," but this man didn't. This man also had red hair, and guys with red hair don't usually call each other "Red.") He said, "John, you've got four boys, and I don't have any. I don't have any children at all. My wife and I wish we had kids. I've got all this money and no one to leave it to. John, why don't you let me take one of your boys and raise him?"

I looked at him with my eyes getting wider and wider! I wasn't sure whether he was serious, but deep down, I thought he was. I still think so today. My younger brother was with me and my dad that day—a couple of towheaded little boys. This man pointed over at me and said, "John, let me take that boy and raise him. I'll give him the best education; I'll give him everything that money can possibly buy."

My dad looked down at me. My dad was a poor man. He looked at me, and then he looked back at the man. The man looked down at me and said, "Son, I'll tell you what. To start off with [he handed me a dollar], I'll give you one dollar every day for an allowance." That was a lot of money to me! Once in a while I got a nickel or sometimes a dime. A dollar a day! I'd heard that some kids got a dollar a week, but I didn't know any of them. He said, "I'll give you a dollar every single day. And when you grow up some day, the automobile dealership will be yours."

My dad was always worried about providing enough for his family. I looked at him, and I could tell that this discussion was causing him to be in a bit of turmoil. I looked at the man, and I walked over and took hold of my dad's hand and said, "No, thanks. I'd better stay with my dad." We got in the old pickup and drove away.

You know something, I never had a second thought about that whole strange incident. In fact, I would have been real upset if my dad had even suggested that he or I might have seriously considered the man's offer. It's a love relationship, you see. It's family with family, friends with friends. A relationship of love.

Jesus ended by saying, " 'These things I have spoken to you, that in Me you may have peace. In the world you will have tribulation; but be of good cheer, I have overcome the world' " (verse 33). With love comes peace. When we are in a love relationship with Jesus, we will have peace no matter what happens in life.

Following Jesus may not be easy. But in spite of all that the devil throws in our way, we will overcome because Jesus has overcome. And we are in Him.

THE LORD'S PRAYER

For seven fantastic years, I had the privilege of serving as senior pastor of the Arlington, Texas, Seventh-day Adventist Church. What a great group of people! It was a real joy to be with them. One year, I preached the entire twelve months from the Gospel of John. That series I preached in Arlington is the foundation for the books I've written on the fourth Gospel.

The only chapter I didn't cover in that series was John 17. I couldn't preach on this sacred chapter then, and at the time of this writing, I still haven't. This chapter is just so sacred I couldn't preach on it; I could only read it prayerfully. I was recently surprised to learn that a number of the classical preachers of the past felt the same way, so I find myself in good company. (That is probably one of the few things that the great preachers and I have in common, because I am certainly not one of them!)

Martin Luther said of Jesus' prayer recorded in John 17, "This is truly, beyond measure, a warm and hearty prayer. He [Jesus] opens the depths of His heart, both in reference to us and to His Father, and He pours them all out. It sounds so honest, so simple: it is so deep, so rich, so wide, no one can fathom it."[1]

Melanchthon, Luther's friend and colleague, wrote, "There is no voice which has ever been heard, either in heaven or in earth, more exalted, more holy, more fruitful, more sublime, than the prayer offered up by the Son to God Himself."[2]

The Scottish Reformer, John Knox, had this prayer read to him every day during his final sickness, and in the closing moments of his life he testified that these verses continued to be a great comfort and a source of strength to him. Philipp Jakob Spener, German theologian and Reformer, had this prayer read to him three times on his deathbed. I could go on and on, naming theologians such as Augustine, Johann Bengel, and others who were deeply affected by this prayer.

Even though the language in John 17 is very simple, the truths are so deep that when you begin to dissect them, you find it is very difficult to do so. Certainly, the whole chapter can't be properly covered in one sermon or really even in a series of sermons. The thoughts presented here will only scratch the surface.

I've called this chapter "The Lord's Prayer." I realize that we normally give that title to the model prayer Christ gave His disciples. However, this prayer in John 17 is the most complete prayer of Jesus recorded in the Bible; truly, it is His prayer—the Lord's Prayer. In it, the Savior prays for Himself, for the eleven remaining disciples, and for all believers—which includes you and me. We will look at some

1. A. W. Pink, ed., *A. W. Pink's Study in the Scriptures: 1926–1927* (Mulberry, Ind.: Sovereign Grace Publishers, 2001), 194.

2. Ibid.

of the highlights, but I invite you to make a deeper study of this chapter in your devotional time.

> Jesus spoke these words, lifted up His eyes to heaven, and said: "Father, the hour has come. Glorify Your Son, that Your Son also may glorify You, as You have given Him authority over all flesh, that He should give eternal life to as many as You have given Him. And this is eternal life, that they may know You, the only true God, and Jesus Christ whom You have sent. I have glorified You on the earth. I have finished the work which You have given Me to do. And now, O Father, glorify Me together with Yourself, with the glory which I had with You before the world was" (John 17:1–5).

Jesus begins this prayer in such a simple manner. Sometimes, we think that in order to pray we have to use Shakespearean English or sound like the King James Bible. We think we have to change our voice and sound spiritual. As an intern pastor, I had the pleasure of working with some very fine preachers. One of them labored with me about my prayers. He told me that they were too simple and common. He gave me an assignment to write out my prayers, using the Psalms and incorporating some very spiritual-sounding language. He talked to me about modulating my voice and about using deeper tones. Now I loved to hear this man pray and preach. He had a very rich voice, and when he prayed, he sounded like Charlton Heston reading the Scriptures for some videos. But when I tried it, I felt like a first-class phony, and soon I went back to just talking to the Lord.

How relieved I was when I read John 17 and found that Jesus just opens His mouth without using a lot of fancy words. He says simply, "Father, the hour has come." He just starts talking to His Father, and that tells me that I can come to the Father, in the name of Jesus too. I can call Him *Abba,* which is a very informal, loving name for the Father, like "Daddy."

Jesus then says that He is being glorified by going to the cross and dying for you and me and everyone who will believe on Him. He says that by this sacrificial gift He is giving us life eternal. Even more, we are adopted into His family, as sons and daughters of the Father.

The apostle Paul wrote in Galatians 6:14, "God forbid that I should glory, save in the cross of our Lord Jesus Christ" (KJV). Now there are many things that Paul could have gloried in. He could have gloried in the pre-existence of Christ; Christ never had a beginning. When He was born in Bethlehem's manger, that was not His beginning; that was His incarnation. Paul could have gloried in the power of Christ; Christ spoke the world into existence. He could have gloried in the teachings, the miracles, and even the resurrection of Christ, but he didn't. He said, "I glory in the cross of Christ."

Why? Because the primary reason Christ came into the world was not to be born, to teach, or to perform miracles. He came into the world for one specific purpose—to go the cross as the Lamb of God and take away the sins of the world. Ever since the Garden of Eden, when the first sacrifice was made pointing forward to His sacrifice on the cross, history had been moving in this direction.

This prayer in John 17 is often called "the High Priestly Prayer" of Jesus. It gives us a little insight into the ministry of Jesus Christ in the sanctuary in heaven where He now ministers in intercession for each believer. The prayer is divided into three parts: First, Jesus prays for Himself. Then He prays for His disciples. And finally, He prays for all believers, including you and me.

As we read the prayer, halfway through the portion in which He prays for the disciples, we find the identifying characteristics of a born-again Christian and of God's church. There are at least seven of these characteristics.

The first is *belief in Jesus,* belief that He was sent from God as our Savior. Jesus says, " 'I have given to them the words which You have given Me; and they have received them, and have known surely that I came forth from You; and they have believed that You sent Me' " (John 17:8). Nothing seems to please God more than faith, belief, and trust in Him.

This belief must start with God as Creator. We learn early in the Bible that God created the world; in fact, we learn that in the very first verse of the very first book. But it doesn't end there. The idea of God as the Creator is prevalent throughout the Bible, including the New Testament where we learn that Jesus Christ was the active One of the Trinity in creating our world. Here are just a few New Testament texts pointing out that Jesus was the Creator:

All things were made through Him [Jesus Christ], and without Him nothing was made that was made (John 1:3).

God who created all things through Jesus Christ (Ephesians 3:9).

For by Him [Jesus Christ] all things were created that are in heaven and that are on earth, visible and invisible, whether thrones or dominions or principalities or powers. All things were created through Him and for Him. And He is before all things, and in Him all things consist (Colossians 1:16, 17).

[God] has in these last days spoken to us by His Son, whom He has appointed heir of all things, through whom also He made the worlds (Hebrews 1:2).

"Worship Him who made heaven and earth, the sea and springs of water" (Revelation 14:7).

Hebrews 11:3 says, "By faith we understand that the worlds were framed by the word of God, so that the things which are seen were not made of things which are visible." Jesus has the right to save us because He is our Creator. If you begin to try to get around Creation with some kind of theory of evolution, you are denying the plan of salvation as well. Those who think that they can believe in evolution and not have it affect their belief in Christ as Savior are sadly mistaken.

Belief and faith go hand in hand. The Bible is clear that without faith and belief in God, we cannot have a relationship with Him. "Without faith it is impossible to please Him [God], for he who comes to God must believe that He is, and that He is a rewarder of those who diligently seek Him" (Hebrews 11:6).

In order to build that belief, God spoke to human beings through His law, which tells us what He is like. Then He spoke to us through His prophets, individuals to whom He gave special and personal direction. And then, last of all and greatest of all, He spoke to us through His Son, who came to show us what God is like. He came to show God's matchless love by taking our place in death, dying for our transgressions on the cross.

When Moses, Elijah, and Christ met on the mount of transfiguration, it was the summation of God's attempt to communicate His love for humankind. On that mountain, God set His seal of approval on His Son, Jesus. He said, " 'This is My beloved Son, in whom I am well pleased. Hear Him!' " (Matthew 17:5). " 'For God so loved the world that He gave His only begotten Son, that whoever believes in Him should not perish but have everlasting life' " (John 3:16). *Belief* is the first characteristic in Jesus' prayer of a true follower of Christ.

The second characteristic may surprise you; it did me. Jesus continued His prayer, saying, " 'Now I come to You, and these things I speak in the world, that they may have My joy fulfilled in themselves' " (John 17:13). We are all familiar with Jesus as a "Man of sorrows and acquainted with grief" (Isaiah 53:3), but several times during His ministry on this earth, Jesus speaks of our having His joy. For example, " 'These things I have spoken to you, that My joy may remain in you, and that your joy may be full' " (John 15:11). Have you noticed that He never seems to mention that He wants us to have His sorrow and His grief, but He does want us to have His joy?

I remember two young brothers who gave their lives to Jesus during a series of meetings I held some years ago in Connecticut. When I came back to that church about a year later as a guest speaker, one of those brothers was still attending church, but the other was not. I asked what had happened, and the faithful brother said, "He died [spiritually] of boredom. He gave up all the things he used to do, and there was no fun in his life anymore."

Christ did not come to take all the fun out of life; He came to give us real, true joy, His joy! The Christian life must not be characterized by just "not doing things." We must plug into a relationship with our Lord that becomes more exciting than anything the world has to offer, a relationship that replaces those things that are "fun" for a season, but are not lasting.

With all the difficulties that the apostle Paul experienced in his life, he still could write a letter to the Philippian believers that mentions the words *joy* and *rejoice* or synonyms nineteen times. Nothing is more exciting than a connection with the God of the universe. Jesus knew this, and He wanted all believers to have the same connection with the Father that He had. "Oh," you say, "but He was God in the flesh, so it was easy for Him to have that connection with the Father." Yes, but don't forget that He was God in the *flesh*. He was God, but He was also human. And He has made it possible for every single one of us to have the same connection with God that He had. The Holy Spirit is with you and in you to facilitate that wonderful experience.

I am writing this chapter in the home of my father- and mother-in-law, Roy and Venice Thurmon. At present, they are ninety-five and ninety-four years old respectively! My wife, Camille, is here for a few days, helping her mom, who recently had a fall. When my wife was a little girl, her family was not Seventh-day Adventist. They belonged to another Christian denomination. Over the last fifty years, I've had the privilege of observing them as they have discovered the real truth of a loving Savior that has brought them a genuine, deep joy. The truth about God and His Son, Jesus, has brought joy and peace into their lives, even in these declining years of pain.

Dad Thurmon said to me recently, "You cannot imagine what joy and peace it brought into our lives when we discovered the truth that God would not torment sinners throughout endless ages. It is impossible to fear God and truly love Him at the same time." That, my friend, is the *joy* of Jesus. It's joy to know God, and we come to know Him by looking at Jesus through the Word of God.

So it shouldn't surprise us that Jesus would say that joy is one of the characteristics of a Christian and of His church. If you don't see joy, you don't see the fruit of the Spirit in that person or in that church. "The fruit of the Spirit is love, joy, peace, longsuffering, kindness, goodness, faithfulness, gentleness, self-control. Against such there is no law" (Galatians 5:22, 23).

The third characteristic of a born-again Christian that we find in Jesus' prayer is *holiness.* Now, I would have thought holiness would be the first characteristic since it is the most mentioned attribute of God in the pages of the Bible. In fact, the Bible says that without holiness, "no one will see the Lord" (Hebrews 12:14).

So, what is holiness? Sometimes we get the idea that holiness means we don't drink, smoke, or "honky-tonk" around. Of course, that's true. Those who have a living relationship with Christ will avoid such things. However, just living this way doesn't guarantee holiness. I've known atheists who had pleasing personalities and whose lifestyles— based on outward appearances—would make you think they were wonderful Christians, but they didn't believe in God or Christ at all. I've known professional athletes who had no faith in God, yet they lived temperate lives that would be an example to anyone. So God must want something better from us. Holiness is not disciplined legalism or a "form of godliness but denying its power" (2 Timothy 3:5). True holiness comes from God and is always God-centered, not man-centered or even performance-centered.

OK, you and I are believers. But in Revelation 3 we find that Jesus Christ, speaking through this same apostle John, says that we are also Laodicea. We like things to be comfortable and are not really committed to Him. We don't really have holiness, either as individuals or as a church. That's kind of discouraging. But then Jesus tells us how to have this holiness. He says, " ' "I counsel you to buy from Me gold refined in the fire, that you may be rich" ' " (Revelation 3:18). What is this gold and where is it found? In Psalm 19, David compares God's Word and His statutes to gold. He says, "More to be desired are they than gold, yea, than much fine gold" (verse 10). When Jesus says that we are to buy from Him gold refined in the fire, it suggests to me that we should "mine" the Word of God for the spiritual riches to be found there. It suggests to me that this experience of holiness with God does not come except as we spend much time with Him in prayerful study of His Word. This makes me ashamed of the pitiful amount of time I have spent with the Word in my life.

Next, Jesus counsels us to buy from Him " ' "white garments, that you may be clothed, that the shame of your nakedness may not be revealed" ' " (Revelation 3:18). We must not come to the banquet without the wedding garment of Christ's righteousness. No matter how good we are—or think we are—we cannot stand before God in our own righteousness. We must have the righteousness of

Christ, which He has promised to give us if we will only ask for it.

Finally, our Lord counsels us to make contact with the Third Person of the Godhead, the Holy Spirit. He says, " ' "Anoint your eyes with eye salve, that you may see" ' " (verse 18). If we really want spiritual insight, we must be led by the Holy Spirit. We must have the anointing of God's Holy Spirit if we are going to walk in His truth.

Whole books could be written on each of these three items—gold, white clothing, and eye salve. Just reading Revelation 3:14–22 should bring us to our knees as we see our need of the holiness Jesus offers. But then, after pointing out our need, the Lord speaks these comforting, reassuring words, " ' "As many as I love, I rebuke and chasten. Therefore be zealous and repent. Behold, I stand at the door and knock. If anyone hears My voice and opens the door, I will come in to him and dine with him, and he with Me" ' " (verses 19, 20). If we are tenderhearted and sensitive to the leading of the Holy Spirit, we will often feel that He chastens us. It is our daily privilege to respond to that chastening and open the doors to our hearts when the Savior knocks.

The fourth characteristic of a born-again Christian in Jesus' prayer is *truth*. " 'Sanctify them by Your truth. Your word is truth' " (John 17:17). The truth is found in Jesus and in Him alone, because He *is* the truth. He says, " 'I am the way, the truth, and the life' " (John 14:6). A friend of mine, when I would say something that was accurate, would often respond by saying, "True and also correct." I liked that, because truth is always correct.

Today, especially here in America, it seems to me that there is almost an abhorrence of the truth. Society today seems to place a premium on fiction, make-believe, and error, not only in books but also in doctrine. Take the Lord's Sabbath, for example. I know of several "big name" pastors of Sunday keeping churches who know without question that Saturday, the seventh day of the week, is the Sabbath of the Bible. They know the Sabbath has never been changed, but they will not share that information with their congregations—either because they don't want to lose their jobs or because they don't want to offend someone. Some of them even secretly keep the Sabbath themselves! I'm certainly glad that the Reformers and those who were burned at the stake for truth didn't have that attitude.

You could make a long list of truths that are clearly taught in God's Word, which are ignored in some churches that teach just the opposite of what the Bible says—ignoring a dozen texts that teach the truth about a subject, focusing instead on one obscure text that seems to say what they want to believe. Spinning the truth so that it becomes some-thing popular and accepted by the world.

We need to stand strong for the truth. We need to rely on the authority of the Word of God. We need to make sure all our teachings are grounded on a biblical founda-tion. We need to have priorities that are Spirit-led and a lifestyle that properly reflects life in Christ. Jesus says that He is "the truth" so we should begin and end all belief, the-ology, and teaching with Him. The truth will be not be absent in the life of a Christian or a church that is Christ-centered.

The next characteristic of a true Christian or church is *evangelism*. " 'As You sent Me into the world, I also have sent them into the world. And for their sakes I sanctify Myself, that they also may be sanctified by the truth' " (John 17:18, 19).

I was at the Tyrone Square Mall in St. Petersburg, Florida. Camille was doing some shopping, and I decided to get some exercise by walking around the corridor of the mall. I was making my second round-trip when I met a man carrying a large shopping bag and some shirts on hangers over his shoulder. "They just put a bunch of shirts on sale for ninety-nine cents at JCPenney!" he almost shouted at me. I went into the store, and sure enough, some shirts that had been thirty-five dollars or more were now just ninety-nine cents! It was a manager's special. I bought some shirts for my sons, Jim Jr. and John, for my son-in-law, Kirk Krueger, and a few for myself. I left the store, and as I walked down the mall corridor, I said to several men that I met, "Hey, they have shirts on sale for ninety-nine cents at Penney's!" You see, I couldn't keep the good news to myself. And that is what Jesus wants us to do as we spread the gospel.

Just tell others what He has done for you! The first book on John that I wrote, which had highlights from the first twelve chapters of John, was dedicated to my daughter Amy and her husband, Ethan. Ethan grew up in a religious Jewish family. Over the years, many rabbis came from their family, and his great-grandfather helped found one of the larger synagogues in Minneapolis. When Ethan was young, his family traveled to Trinidad and Tobago, an island nation off of the coast of Venezuela. His father had combined a vacation with business; it was then that Ethan met a man named Arthur Isaac, a faithful Seventh-day Adventist Christian who befriended Ethan's father. This man became a great friend to this young Jewish boy, and Ethan would later say, "He was my second father." Ethan saw in Arthur the characteristics Jesus prayed that His followers would have. He saw a man who believed, who had peaceful joy, who demonstrated holiness and truth, and it made a very positive impact on him.

Later, Ethan became acquainted with another Adventist Christian, and they would spend hours talking about spiritual things. Then Ethan met Amy. It was about as close to love at first sight as you can get, and the events that caused their paths to cross were too unbelievable to have been accidental. They were married. Ethan again had come into close contact with Adventists—not only Amy, but all of her family, including Amy's grandfather, Pastor Roy Thurmon. In time, Ethan began to study about Jesus on his own, especially Matthew 5, 6, and 7—the Sermon on the Mount. They moved to California from Dallas and began to attend the little Soquel church. Those folks took Amy, Ethan, and their young son, Levi, under their wings and loved them. They even asked Ethan to have the sermon. He was not yet baptized and had made no profession of belief in Jesus, but they showed him love and confidence; and it paid big dividends. He told about his journey, and at the end he announced that he had accepted Jesus Christ as his Savior and had called me to set the date for his baptism when all of our family could be present.

That all started with Arthur Isaac's witness.

You can preach all day, and at 3ABN, we do—24-7. But the most powerful sermon is a life full of the joy of Jesus! That translates even over the airwaves!

The sixth characteristic of a genuine Christian and his church is *unity*. Jesus said,

"I do not pray for these alone, but also for those who will believe in Me through their word; that they all may be one, as You, Father, are in Me, and I in You; that they also may be one in Us, that the world may believe that You sent Me. And the glory which You gave Me I have given them, that they may be one just as We are one: I in them, and You in Me; that they may be made perfect in one, and that the world may know that You have sent Me, and have loved them as You have loved Me" (John 17:20–23).

When Jesus was on this earth, the disciples never achieved this kind of unity. But at Pentecost, the Bible says, "They were all with one accord in one place" (Acts 2:1). They finally had unity of purpose. And what happened? The Holy Spirit came and filled them with power!

Clearly, Jesus isn't speaking here of organizational unity. The church had organizational unity during the Middle Ages: one church with a pope at its head. But was the church spiritually strong and filled with faith during this time? No. It did more damage to true faith than the opposition did! This was not the unity for which the Lord prayed. He prayed not for conformity but for unity in diversity—spiritual unity.

The unity that Jesus wants us to have is unity with Him and with the Father. And when we have this unity with Him through the Word and through prayer, we will find unity with our brothers and sisters who are having the same experience. Yes, we may have differences of opinion. Unity doesn't mean uniformity. But there will be a oneness of spirit, a unity of love and purpose that comes from our common connection with Jesus and the Father. We don't need to focus on trying to get along with one another; we need to focus on getting along with the Father, the Son, and the Holy Spirit. And the result will be unity in spirit with like believers.

Don't think for a moment that this will bring harmony with the world; it definitely will not. It didn't for Jesus, and it won't for you and me. It will also not make all of us believers agree on everything and conform to one another. It will, however, help us to be able to get along with each other even when we disagree.

The seventh and last characteristic of a born-again Christian is *love*. " 'O righteous Father!' " Jesus prayed, " 'The world has not known You, but I have known You; and these have known that You sent Me. And I have declared to them Your name, and will declare it, that the love with which You loved Me may be in them, and I in them' " (verses 25, 26).

Which of these seven characteristics is the greatest? I don't mean which one is named first, although you would have to say that *belief* needs to be right up there at the top of the list. But Paul makes it clear in 1 Corinthians 13 that love surpasses all else. And John agrees. In John 13:34, 35 and all through his little book of 1 John, he agrees with Paul that love is the characteristic that is most important in the Christian's life and in the church.

Take love away from belief, and you have nothing except a lot of noise, Paul says. Take love away from joy, and you end up with some kind of hedonism. Holiness without love becomes legalism. Truth without love becomes orthodoxy. Unity without love becomes tyranny.

However, when you find love—true love, not some kind of phony, counterfeit love that is used to manipulate people—you will soon find joy and all of the other characteristics Christ prayed for His disciples to have. His prayer included both the eleven disciples who were left after Judas departed *and* all the millions of those who would accept Jesus as their Lord and Savior—including you and me.

Jesus Christ has made it clear that if we don't have love, then we do not know God, for God is love. "Beloved, let us love one another, for love is of God; and everyone who loves is born of God and knows God. He who does not love does not know God, for God is love" (1 John 4:7, 8).

I am so glad that John recorded this prayer of Jesus, even though the other Gospels seem to indicate that the disciples were very sleepy at the time. I'm also grateful to the Holy Spirit for keeping these words alive in John's memory until he could write them down. Truly, it deserves to be known as the "Lord's Prayer." It's the most beautiful and complete prayer of Jesus found anywhere in Scripture. It's a great complement to the model prayer that begins "Our Father which art in heaven . . ." (Matthew 6:9, KJV). It's the Lord's prayer for Himself, His disciples, and for you and me.

VOLUME III

IN THE GARDEN

So far, we've seen Jesus washing the feet of the disciples in the upper room, giving them an unparalleled example of humility and service (John 13). We've heard His last words to His disciples—all the important things He needed to say to them, and us, before His death (John 14, 15, and 16). We've listened to His prayer to the Father for the eleven disciples who were with Him that night and for those disciples who would come after them, including you and me (John 17). We've been deeply impressed by that prayer. Now, we come to the eighteenth chapter of John's Gospel, and we find the final events of the Master's earthly ministry beginning to unfold swiftly. John writes that when Jesus finished His prayer, "He went out with His disciples over the Brook Kidron, where there was a garden, which He and His disciples entered" (John 18:1).

Now, John doesn't go into all the details of what happened there in the Garden of Gethsemane, because by the time he wrote, Matthew, Mark, and Luke had already written their Gospels and had told the story of what happened there. John's narrative moves right into the events surrounding Judas's betrayal and Jesus' arrest. You may remember that the other three Gospel writers tell how Jesus left all of the disciples, except Peter, James, and John, near the entrance to the garden. He asked these three men to go with Him farther into the garden and to join Him in prayer. They tried to do as He asked, but they were so tired and sleepy! They tried to stay awake. They would pray a little while and then doze off. Then wake up and pray a little longer before going back to sleep. Have you ever done that? Praying and dozing and praying and dozing? Fighting sleep and trying to stay awake?

Peter, James, and John wanted to support Jesus, but it seemed they just couldn't stay awake. They knew He was under extreme emotional stress, but they didn't know why. They didn't understand at all the stupendous battle Christ was fighting there in the Garden. He went a little farther into the garden all by Himself and knelt and prayed in agony of spirit to His Father. The Bible says that He actually sweat blood (see Luke 22:44). Medical experts tell us that this is something that is literally possible under severe strain and stress. It happened to Jesus. The Savior was carrying the heaviest load that anyone has ever carried or ever will carry on this earth, because He was carrying the guilt of every single sin that you and I and all of us have ever done. The guilt of all the combined sins of the entire world was placed on Him. The Bible says, "Surely He has borne our griefs and carried our sorrows. . . . And the LORD has laid on Him the iniquity of us all" (Isaiah 53:4, 6).

It began in that garden. That's where Jesus began to feel the guilt and the weight of our sins. And those sins began to separate Him from His Father. This was something He had never felt before—the separation from God that sin causes.

As sinners, we're used to it. We know how it feels when our sins push us away from God and separate us from Him. We know that sense of not being close to God because of something we've done that we shouldn't have done. But this was something Jesus had never known before. He had always relied so completely upon the close, inseparable connection between Himself and His Father. Now, that connection was being broken up, and Jesus was in agony. The guilt and sin that had been placed on Him was crushing out His life. He felt hopeless, lost, and utterly cut off from His Father. He longed for some support from His friends, but they were asleep.

And then, just when it seemed that things were about as bad as they could be, Judas showed up with "a detachment of troops, and officers from the chief priests and Pharisees, . . . with lanterns, torches, and weapons" (John 18:3). Judas had betrayed his Master. He had sold Him to the priests for thirty pieces of silver. Though if you stop to think about it, Judas didn't sell Jesus; actually, he sold himself. That's what he did. He placed a price upon himself, upon his loyalty, his integrity, and his eternal destiny. And the value he placed on all that was only thirty pieces of silver! Judas sold himself cheap. We think, *I'd never do that.* But sometimes we do. Sometimes we sell ourselves for a whole lot less than that—a slightly better job, a little recognition and status, and a little more power or influence. We can deny our Lord and sell our souls for many different reasons. It can happen over a long period of time, or it can happen in the blink of an eye—as Peter found out to his great sorrow.

You remember how Peter insisted that he would never deny Jesus. The Master had told the disciples, " 'All of you will be made to stumble because of Me this night' "

(Matthew 26:31). "Not me," Peter declared. "I'll never deny You. I don't know about these other disciples; maybe they will stumble and deny You. But I won't. I'd die first!" And then all the rest of the disciples chimed in and insisted that they, too, would never deny their Master (see verses 33–35). How little they knew themselves! How little it actually took to cause all of them to run away in the garden!

How little we know our own hearts as well. When everything is going well and there is no opposition or persecution or trouble, it's easy to say, "I would never deny You, Lord. You can count on me." But then a little opposition comes along, and before we know what has happened, we've denied the Lord with a word or an action. That's what Peter did.

Peter's name wasn't really *Peter,* you know. His real name was *Simon.* Peter was a name Jesus gave him; it means "rock" (see John 1:42). Peter is called "Simon Bar-Jonah" in Matthew 16:17, meaning "Simon, the son of John." Today, we'd probably call him "Simon Johnson." Or with the nickname Jesus gave him, he would be "Rocky Johnson." How did "the Rock" do there in the Garden when the chips were down? Well, he tried. You've got to give Peter credit for trying. The record says that when Judas came with the soldiers and officers of the priests to arrest Jesus, "Simon Peter, having a sword, drew it and struck the high priest's servant, and cut off his right ear" (John 18:10).

Peter had told Jesus, "I'll die before I deny you." And now he is ready to prove it by giving his life to defend his Master. Peter reached down inside his robe somewhere and whipped out a knife—not a long sword like a Roman soldier might carry, but a long, thin dagger. He drew that weapon and lunged for the nearest person, who happened to be a man named Malchus, a servant of the high priest. Peter sliced off the man's right ear, and the only reason he got an ear instead of slicing through his jugular vein was because the fellow must have instinctively jerked away when Peter came at him with that dagger. Peter meant business; he was ready to fight for Jesus. He was ready to prove what he had said earlier—"I will never forsake You."

But Peter missed the whole idea. Everything was unfolding according to plan—the eternal plan of salvation determined in heaven from the beginning. This was the reason Jesus had left heaven and come to earth. " 'Put your sword into the sheath,' " Jesus told Peter. " 'Shall I not drink the cup which My Father has given Me?' " (verse 11). The way I imagine it, Jesus thoughtfully reached down and picked up Malchus's ear off the ground. Maybe He had to brush off some bits of dirt and grass that were sticking to the rapidly drying blood. And He reached over and placed the ear back on the side of the man's head and healed him (see Luke 22:51)!

Poor Peter! He had thought he was doing the right thing. He thought he was bravely standing up for Jesus and defending Him to the death. *Lord,* he must have thought, *I said I would stand with You no matter what. I've stood up for You, and now You're rebuking me? You're telling me to back off? What is going on? I don't understand!* Peter was confused, and then he became frightened. And he and the other disciples took to their heels and ran away into the darkness of the garden, away from the torches and the soldiers and the danger, leaving Jesus to face the mob alone.

Let's not be too hard on Peter and the others. Peter had tried to defend Jesus. But Jesus didn't react the way Peter expected Him to. Before, when confrontation took place,

Jesus would just disappear into the crowd and slip away. But this time He stepped forward. He seemed to accept what was happening. So Peter lost heart and ran away. That's easy to do when the Lord isn't responding to us the way we are expecting Him to—when we think we're taking a stand for Him, and it all turns wrong. Has that ever happened to you? Peter really intended to stand up for Jesus, but his courage left him when Jesus seemed to accept the situation.

And, of course, Jesus *did* accept what was taking place. It was time. He had come for this very time—to go to the cross. He had prayed for strength to drink the cup, and now the time had come. "Then the detachment of troops and the captain and the officers of the Jews arrested Jesus and bound Him. And they led Him away" (John 18:12, 13).

When a Roman soldier took you prisoner, he would reach for you, stomp down hard on your instep, and whirl you around with your hand behind your back. Then he would grab your other hand and bring it behind your back as well. This was standard procedure, and no doubt the soldier arresting Jesus used this painful technique with Him. His arrest started with pain; it continued in pain; and it ended in pain. Jesus didn't struggle; He didn't resist. As the prophet Isaiah had predicted so many years before, "He was led as a lamb to the slaughter" (Isaiah 53:7).

The soldiers took Jesus first to Annas, the former high priest and the father-in-law of Caiaphas, the current high priest. Why would they take Jesus to Annas, the ex-high priest, and not to Caiaphas who currently held the office? They did so, because even though Annas was not then the high priest, he was still the great Jewish power broker—the power behind the throne.

Maybe you remember that early in John's Gospel he tells how Jesus made a little whip of cords and ran the money changers and the livestock dealers out of the temple (see John 2:13–22). Jesus' troubles with the religious leaders of Israel began with that incident. You see, the priests and leaders had a good thing going. They completely controlled all the sacrifices in the temple. Let's say you are a Jew from northern Galilee, coming to offer a lamb in the temple at Jerusalem. You've brought your own lamb with you. The priests would inspect your animal. After all, God's law said that a sacrificial animal must be without blemish. You could be sure that the priests would find a blemish on your lamb! It would never pass inspection. Of course, they would be happy to sell you a preapproved lamb—at three or four times the going rate. Meanwhile, what were you going to do with the lamb you had brought all the way from northern Galilee? You didn't want to have to take it all the way back home. Maybe you could sell it. Reluctantly, the priests would agree to take it off your hands—for a low price, of course, since it was "blemished." But if you came back to the temple the next day, you would probably see your "blemished" lamb in the "preapproved" pen, waiting to be sold to another worshiper.

The reason there were money changers in the temple was because all offerings had to be made using the "temple shekel." If you had come from some distant part of the world and didn't happen to have any temple shekels, that wasn't a problem. The money changers were happy to exchange your money into temple shekels—at an exchange rate very favorable to themselves. It's no wonder Jesus drove these rascals out of the temple and said they had made it into a den of thieves! This kind of corruption was prevalent.

The office of high priest had become a political plum, a lucrative position of power and corruption. If you belonged to the right family, if you could walk the thin line between the religious and the irreligious, if you could live with corruption and wrong and be a part of it, then you could thrive and prosper as high priest. Annas had done it quite successfully and had then passed the office to his sons and now to his son-in-law, Caiaphas, and he was still the power behind the throne. Annas may have been high priest when Christ had thrown out the money changers and livestock dealers, interrupting and exposing his corruption. And I can imagine the high priest saying to himself, "I'll get You for this someday!" Maybe that's why the soldiers took Jesus first to Annas.

After questioning Jesus, Annas sent Him to his son-in-law, Caiaphas, for more interrogation. Then they took Him to the Sanhedrin. These first three "trials" were all quick, illegal, and carried out by the Jewish leaders. Then Jesus was taken to Pilate, the Roman governor of Judea. Pilate was already in hot water with Rome. He was trying to stay in power by straddling the fence—doing whatever he could to keep both Rome and the Jews happy. When Jesus appeared before him, Pilate said to the Jews, "Why are you bringing this Man to me? Why don't you try Him and take care of this?"

"Because," they answered, "we can't put Him to death, but you can."

Now earlier that night, during His questioning before the Jews, the big issue was blasphemy. But when they brought Jesus to Pilate, they accused Him of treason. They knew the Roman court could not care less about the charge of blasphemy. So they accused Him of treason. "He claims to be a king," they told Pilate. "He wants to overthrow Rome."

Pilate talked to Jesus and came out to tell the Jewish leaders, " 'I find no fault in Him at all' " (John 18:38).

"You can't let Him go," they shouted. "He's caused insurrection and trouble all over Galilee!"

"Is He a Galilean?" Pilate asked eagerly.

"Yes."

"Well, Galilee is Herod's jurisdiction. He's in town right now. Take Him to Herod for judgment."

So they took Jesus to Herod. Herod was happy to see Jesus—not because he wanted to pass judgment on Him, but because he had heard a lot about Jesus and he wanted to see Jesus perform a miracle. Herod was really into miracles and magic tricks. He tried to get Christ to perform a miracle, but He refused. Again, the mob and the soldiers mistreated and mocked Jesus. And then Herod, disappointed that Jesus didn't satisfy his curiosity, returned Him to Pilate without making any kind of decision about Him.

All this time, Peter had been thinking about what was happening. When he ran away in the garden that night, he didn't run very far. He slipped along in the darkness behind the mob as they led Jesus off to be questioned by Annas. Peter, along with John, slipped into the courtyard of the ex-high priest and tried to mingle unnoticed with the people who were hanging around there. Among them, Peter saw a relative of Malchus, the man whose ear he had sliced off a short while earlier. The man looked at Peter and asked, "Aren't you one of them?"

"No! I'm not one of them!"

"But you must be," someone else spoke up. "You sound like a Galilean." And Peter denied it the second time.

A little later, a serving girl asked, " 'You are not also one of this Man's disciples, are you?' " (John 18:17).

"Absolutely not," Peter insisted. And he added a few choice swearwords to clinch his denial. No longer did he sound like one of Jesus' disciples. He sounded like Simon, the fishermen, not like Peter the Rock, the one whom Christ had chosen. Jesus had understood Peter better than he understood himself. Jesus had told Peter that he would deny Him three times that night. And that is just what happened.

Peter was weak. Peter didn't realize how weak he was. But for all his weakness, Peter loved the Lord. When it dawned on him what he had done, he rushed back to the Garden of Gethsemane, eyes blinded by tears, repenting bitterly of his sin and wishing he could die. That was the great difference between Peter and Judas. Judas "repented" too. He became sorry he had betrayed Jesus—sorry that things hadn't turned out as he had intended, but not sorry for his sin. Deep down, Judas didn't love Jesus; he loved Judas. Peter was a weak sinner, but he loved Jesus. And he was sorry he had denied Him—not for his own sake, but for the hurt it had brought to his beloved Master. Jesus knew Peter's heart. And He knows your heart too. When we hurt Him, He knows whether we do it thoughtlessly, in weakness, or whether we do it intentionally, calculating the odds. He forgave Peter, and He will forgive us.

Herod sent Jesus back to Pilate, who was not happy to see this Man return. Pilate did everything he could to find Jesus innocent, but the Jewish leaders would not accept it. Pilate thought he could offer them a choice between Jesus and Barabbas and that they surely would not choose to release the hardened criminal, Barabbas. But they did. "What will I do with Jesus, then?" Pilate asked.

"Crucify Him!" they shouted.

I can image Barabbas nearby in prison. He can hear the crowd. He can't hear the conversation between the Jewish leaders and Pilate, but he can hear the crowd shouting, "Barabbas!" And then a moment or two later, he hears the crowd shouting, "Crucify Him!" Of course, he thinks that the crowd is screaming for his death. How surprised he must have been when the prison guards came to his cell—*and released him*! He thought they were coming to nail him to a cross. And, of course, a few hours later, Roman soldiers *did* crucify a Prisoner—Jesus Christ. Barabbas must have watched Jesus' crucifixion that day with entirely different eyes than anybody else. He had expected to be there on that cross, but someone else was there instead. Someone else had taken his place.

And that's the way you and I need to look at the cross as well. That cross should have been our cross. We deserve to die for our sins. But Jesus took our place. He was tried and found guilty although He was innocent. That's the way it has been for God ever since sin entered His perfect universe. The devil has been accusing Him of things He was not guilty of. The devil is still doing that.

Not long ago, I was with a man who had experienced a great disappointment in his life. He had lost someone very dear to him. He told me, "I am angry with God. I am angry with Jesus. I am angry with the Holy Spirit."

"My friend," I said, "you're angry with the wrong ones. You *should* be angry. You should be angry from the top of your head to the bottom of your feet. But you shouldn't be angry with God; you should be angry with the devil. Let me tell you something: God is angry too. He's angry with the devil, because of the way he treated His Son. God's angry with the devil, because of what he has done to this world. The Bible speaks of the wrath of God, and don't ever believe that God isn't justifiably angry. He's not angry with you and me—poor individuals who are caught up in this mess the devil has created. No, He's not angry with us, but He is angry with the devil, and He's going to bring an end to him and to the sin he has caused. I look forward to the day God does that. It's not over yet. Death isn't ended—yet. Pain isn't ended—yet. It's ended for your loved one, but it's not over for you and me. I look forward to Jesus' return and having Him put an end to sorrow and sin. And He will end it; that's His promise. Sin and death and all the pain and suffering will come to an end."

A young man went to Chicago to go to a Christian school. He wanted a job, but he couldn't find one. He had hoped to find a job working for a church or some kind of a youth ministry or something of that nature, but he found nothing. Then he heard that a company was hiring bus drivers. He prayed about it and decided that the Lord was leading him to this bus-driving job. So he took it. He said, "Lord, I'm using this job to make money to go to school to prepare for the ministry, but I want You to help me to minister even in this job as a bus driver."

The company sent him out to the south side of Chicago. If you know anything about Chicago, you'll know why there was an opening for a bus driver on the south side of the city. Nobody would drive a bus on the south side. But this young man went. After he had been driving for several days, four young punks got on the bus and walked right past him without paying the fare. He told them they needed to pay. They laughed at him and sat in the back of the bus. He drove on.

Day after day, these same four young hoodlums got on the bus at the same stop—without paying. And day after day, the young Christian driver looked for a policeman. "You can never find one when you really need one," he would say to himself. But one day his tormentors got on the bus without paying as usual, and within two blocks, there was a policeman! The driver stopped the bus. He got off and told the policeman, "There are four young men sitting on that bus who get on day after day without paying. They just laugh when I ask them to pay. Please, make them pay—at least today."

The policeman came on the bus, and he made them pay. The young driver was gratified. He sat down behind the wheel, and the policeman got off the bus—and then came the part the young man hadn't thought through. He drove a few blocks and turned a corner, and that was the last thing he remembered. The four delinquents knocked him down and relieved him of several teeth and all his money. When he woke up, they were gone, and the bus was empty. He was very upset. "Lord," he said, "why did You lead me to this place? I prayed for a job where I could work for You and serve others. Why did You lead me here?"

He was able to track down his assailants and have them arrested. He went to court as a witness, and when the judge was getting ready to hand down the sentence, he suddenly realized something. He realized that these four young men needed Christ. He asked the court for permission to speak. The judge granted it. He said, "Judge, I would like for you to add up the total sentence for all four of these young men—and let me take it instead of them!"

"That's impossible," the judge declared. "That's never been done before."

"Oh, yes, it has," the young bus driver said. "Somebody did it two thousand years ago." Then he began to witness about the love of Jesus right there in court. As a result, three of those four defendants accepted Jesus Christ that same day! The judge made the fourth go to jail, and he accepted Jesus after spending some time there. These four former hoodlums joined the bus driver and began an inner-city ministry there on the south side of Chicago.

Sometimes, my friend, we underestimate the power of the gospel of Jesus Christ. We underestimate the power that comes from uplifting our Lord and Savior. He can take your life or my life with all of its disappointments and all the hurts and all that we've done that we shouldn't have done, and He can turn it into something beautiful.

It all stems from the decision He made there in the Garden. The decision to accept the sins of the world, your sins and mine, as if they were His own. The decision to go to the cross and pay the penalty there for our sins so that we could be saved. All you and I have to do is to accept His great sacrifice and ask Him to cover us with His righteousness. He will do it if we ask Him to. After all, that's why He came to earth.

JESUS OR BARABBAS?

A Christian and a Jew were in the same business and became acquainted with each other. Every week or two, they would meet together to eat and talk. Soon their conversations turned toward religion. The Christian man told his Jewish friend all about Jesus and why he believed in Him. His companion just couldn't see it. One day, the Christian began telling his friend the story of Jesus' crucifixion. He told him about Barabbas and the part he played in the story. *Barabbas,* meaning "the son of the father" or "the son of the rabbi," was probably a rabbi's son who had gone bad. The Christian told his Jewish friend of the choice Pilate had given to the people and how they had shouted, "Release Barabbas and crucify Jesus! Let His blood be on us and on our children." Still, the story didn't seem to make much of an impression on the Jewish man.

Word came one day to the Christian businessman that his friend was very sick and in the hospital. He went to see him. Because of his serious condition, the nurses hadn't been letting the sick man have any visitors. But they knew what good friends the two men were, so when the Christian man came to the hospital, they said, "OK, you can go in. But just for a minute or two."

He slipped into the room and found his friend asleep. He was sleeping so soundly that the man didn't want to disturb him. Instead, he knelt by the bed and began whispering a prayer. While he was praying, the sick man woke up and reached over and took his friend's hand. When his friend finished that prayer, the Jewish man said in a weak voice, "I choose Jesus, not Barabbas. I accept Jesus as my King and my Savior." Right there on his deathbed, he accepted Jesus, the Lamb that was slain for his sins and for your sins and for my sins and for the sins of every person who has ever lived.

Jesus Christ died on the cross. John 19 tells us about it— Jesus' condemnation, humiliation, and torture, the crucifixion, and His burial—although I'm sure that John's Gospel tells us only a little of all that happened that terrible day. I'm sure there was much more that he could have recorded. As we look at these awful events, it's important to remember that *the cross was not an accident.* Sometimes people think that Jesus came to this earth for a certain purpose, but somehow everything went astray. That somehow, His plan fell apart and His mission here on earth failed and He went to the cross and died, because things didn't work out for Him the way they were supposed to. Some people believe that and teach that. But that view of the cross simply is not true. At Pentecost, some weeks after Jesus' death, Peter preached to a large crowd in Jerusalem. In his sermon, he said that Jesus' death on the cross took place according to " 'the determined purpose and foreknowledge of God' " (Acts 2:23). There is no question why Jesus came to our world; He came to die on the cross. The Bible had foretold

His death some nine hundred years earlier when David, in the Psalms, wrote about the Messiah's hands and feet being pierced (see Psalm 22:16). The Bible had foretold Jesus' death some seven hundred years earlier when the prophet Isaiah wrote that He would be "wounded for our transgressions" and "bruised for our iniquities" (Isaiah 53:5). He predicted that the Messiah would be "cut off from the land of the living" and be stricken "for the transgressions of My people" (verse 8).

So, it's very clear, my friend, that the Cross was not an accident. There is a moral-based "theology" movement going around today that is trying to do away with the blood of the Cross. That tries to act as if the blood wasn't necessary. This "moral theology" misses the whole point. Jesus came to this earth for the very purpose of shedding His blood on the cross.

I was flying home from somewhere awhile back. I was sitting in the back of the plane because I hoped to get three seats together where I could sit in the middle seat and spread out and put down all three trays and really get some work done. But it didn't work out that way. The plane was full. A lady came back to my row and wanted to sit by the window. As she passed by me, the alcohol fumes from her breath were so strong they cleared my sinuses! I had no more sinus problems for the rest of the flight and for some time thereafter! She sat down, and then she wanted to talk. I had my Bible out on the tray, along with a commentary and some papers. I was studying as best I could, and this woman wanted to tell me about her cat! It was a Siamese, and she told me that she had called Southwest Airlines before the flight and had been assured that if she put the cat in a certain type of airline-approved cage, she could bring it on the plane with her. But when she got to the counter, the agent had said, "We don't take animals." (Some airlines treat people like animals, but that's another subject!)

"Oh, I had a big 'to do' with the agent about that!" she said.

So she went over to Continental Airlines, and the agent there told her, "Well, you can take your cat on the plane, but you'll have to buy it a ticket!"

It was time for her ultimate weapon. "I began to cry," she told me. Now, some people can really turn it on! My brother Paul once told me that I would never be a great preacher. "Why not?" I wanted to know.

"Because you can't cry when you want to and stop crying when you want to. Great preachers can do that." Then he named a few.

This lady apparently could cry when she wanted to! She turned on the tears, and finally got her cat on a Continental plane without buying it a ticket. "I could get fired for this," the Continental agent told her, which didn't seem to bother her at all. Anyway, as best I could make out her story, her cat was on its way to Houston on a Continental plane, and she was going there on a Southwest plane. She eventually forgot about her cat and went to sleep. But during our discussion, the flight attendant came by our row. He looked at me and my books and Bible. "You're studying the Bible," he commented with a sort of question in his voice.

"That's right," I replied.

"Are you a minister?"

"Yes."

"What church?"

"Seventh-day Adventist."

"What are you studying about?"

"The Gospel of John."

He said, "What is John's message?" He said down across the aisle and clearly wanted to talk about the book of John.

"Well," I said, "John's message is simply that Jesus is both God and human. He's one hundred percent God, and He's one hundred percent man."

"That's what I think too," he said.

We had a real good talk about the Gospel of John and spiritual things. I talked to him about the picture of Jesus that John gives us in his book. About how God came to this earth, somehow clothing His deity in human flesh, becoming a human being. About how He was treated as we really deserve to be treated, so that we could be treated as He deserves. We had a great discussion until the flight attendant had to get back to work!

And I began thinking about what I had told him. About the picture of Jesus that appears in John's Gospel. You know, we've heard it so many times that it just runs off us like water off a duck. It doesn't even move us. I'd like to challenge you to read John 19—the story of Jesus' death on the cross—and make it very personal as you read it. Think about how He did all this for *you.* How He would still have done all this for you even if you were the only person on earth that needed salvation! He did it for *you*!

Let's look a little more closely at the situation as John recounts the final events in Jesus' life here on earth.

First, Pilate was dealing with the Jewish religious leaders from a position of weakness. He was in trouble with his superiors—and the Jewish leaders knew it. Shortly after Pilate had arrived to be the governor of this troublesome province of Judea, he had made three mistakes. The capital of the province in Roman times was not Jerusalem, you see, but Caesarea on the Mediterranean Sea. That's where Pilate lived and where the Roman governors before him had lived. The first time Pilate came to visit Jerusalem as governor, he came, of course, with a contingent of Roman soldiers. The regimental standards that these soldiers carried were topped with an emblem on which was a bust of the emperor. Now, all the Roman governors before Pilate had had the sensitivity to take off these emblems with the image of the emperor before entering the holy city of Jerusalem. They knew that the Jews considered the emblems to be graven images and that it was offensive to them to have the soldiers carry these into Jerusalem. So to avoid alienating them, the governors had removed these emblems before entering the city. Not Pilate. He refused to do it.

The Jews were so incensed that when Pilate left Jerusalem, a group of Jews followed him all the way back to Caesarea demanding that he never again bring those emblems of the emperor back to Jerusalem. "You've got to take those off," they insisted. "Don't bring those soldiers back to Jerusalem again carrying those standards with the emperor's image on them."

Well, that made Pilate mad. So he invited all these Jewish protestors to the amphitheater in Caesarea. Then he ringed the amphitheater with soldiers and told the Jews, "If you don't be quiet about this, I'm going to have all of you beheaded right now."

And do you know what those Jewish leaders did? They leaned over, stuck out their necks, and told Pilate, "Go ahead and cut off our heads!" Pilate knew—and they knew—that he couldn't do that. He couldn't just execute all of them. So he backed down and took the image of the emperor off the soldiers' standards whenever they came to Jerusalem. That was the first run-in that Pilate had with the Jews, and he didn't come out of it looking very good.

The second mistake Pilate made as governor of Judea involved the Jerusalem water supply. The city needed a new water system. But it didn't have the money for one. So Pilate took his soldiers to the temple, marched them right inside to the temple treasury and took the necessary funds. Now, the temple treasury contained two kinds of money. There was *corban* money—non-tithe money that could be used for any purpose. The other money in the treasury was tithe money. At least, Pilate took *corban* money to build a new water system in Jerusalem, but the people resented his high-handed ways so much that they picketed the work constantly. They interrupted it every chance they got. They held demonstrations against the water project.

Pilate retaliated by putting some of his soldiers in civilian clothes and having them mingle with the demonstrators to find out who the troublemakers were. Then, at a given moment, he ordered the soldiers to attack the ring leaders. They beat some and killed some. Let me tell you, that *really* caused problems between Pilate and the Jews! Word even got back to Rome about this incident. So Pilate was in trouble. Not only was he in trouble with the Jews in Judea, he was in trouble with his superiors in Rome.

Pilate's third mistake was having some shields made with the image of the emperor on them. I guess he thought, *If I can't put the emperor's image on the soldiers' regimental standards, then I'll put it on their shields.* Pilate just didn't seem to learn! The Jews were furious, of course, and this time word came from Rome, from the emperor himself, "Take my image off the soldiers' shields!"

But Pilate's real problem, his final problem, occurred following Jesus' crucifixion. These three earlier mistakes took place before the Crucifixion. But some time after Jesus was put to death, there was an uprising in Samaria. Now, for the most part, Samaria was generally pro-Rome and anti-Jewish. But there was a minor insurrection in Samaria against the Roman authorities, and Pilate overreacted. He sent in troops and killed a lot of Samaritans. For this, Pilate was called back to Rome to face charges. Fortunately for him, the emperor, Tiberius, died while Pilate was en route to Rome. So as far as we know, he never had to actually account for his actions. But at this point, Pilate disappears from recorded history. There are a lot of ideas and speculation about what happened to him, but the truth is that we simply don't know what took place after that as far as Pilate is concerned.

So, when Pilate faced the Jewish leaders and the crowd that Friday and heard them calling out, demanding that he crucify Jesus, he was in a difficult position. He was straddling the fence, trying to pacify the Jews and yet protect Rome's interest. He could see that Jesus was not actually guilty of any crime, but he decided to have Him scourged, hoping that would satisfy the Jews. "So then Pilate took Jesus and scourged Him" (John 19:1).

A Roman scourging was nothing to take lightly. The scourge was a whip with a wooden handle fourteen to eighteen inches long. Attached to this handle were a number of leather strips. And tied to the end of these strips were sharp pieces of bone, metal, or glass—anything that could tear or rip out flesh. The Jews, as well as the Romans, punished individuals by flogging them. But Deuteronomy 25:2, 3 prohibited the Jews from administering more than forty lashes. In practice, they stopped with thirty-nine to be sure they didn't miscount and break the law by giving more than forty lashes! But the Romans weren't worried at all about how many blows they gave a prisoner. There was no limit as far as they were concerned.

A Roman scourging was carried out by a *lictor,* a specialist in torture. The prisoner was stripped naked and bent over a stump or a low wooden platform—his feet tied to two rings on one side of the stump and his hands tied to two rings on the other side. The *lictor* would begin by beating the upper part of the body, and when the little pieces of metal or bone at the end of the leather strips hit the flesh, they tore out pieces and caused little hemorrhages. You never knew how long the scourging might last. Men sometimes died while they were being beaten; in fact, it was referred to at times as "the halfway death." A person was half dead, at best, when the beating was finished. To revive someone who passed out during the beating, the soldiers would throw a bucket of cold salt water on him. The whole body would be convulsing and teeth chattering by the time the beating was completed.

You don't like to read about this, do you? I don't like it either. But I believe that sometimes we need to take an honest look at what actually happened to our Lord. Pilate let his soldiers scourge Him, and this was what a Roman scourging was like. Most of those whom the Romans scourged deserved to be punished. They had done something that warranted punishment—even if not such a brutal one. But Jesus had done nothing wrong, as even Pilate admitted. He took that terrible beating for you and me. That's what the plan of salvation included—this torture, this shame, this suffering in our place. The plan had been made back in the beginning, long before sin occurred. All heaven was aware of what was going to take place when the Son of God left heaven and came to this earth as a man. I can just imagine the cries of protest from the angels—the unfallen ones. "Oh, don't do that! Don't send the Son of God to earth to suffer that!"[1]

But Jesus *chose* to come and endure all that the plan included. He didn't have to. He could have stayed in heaven. Or He could have given up the struggle and returned to heaven at any time. As the song says, He could have called ten thousand angels to destroy the world and set Him free. He could have, but He chose not to. In answer to His call, the angels would have come to His side in an instant. They would have laid all those Roman soldiers gasping in the dust. But Jesus didn't call for the angels to come and deliver Him. He chose, instead, to die alone for you and me.

Have you ever seen anyone who has really been beaten? One day I got a call to go down to the city jail in Dallas. A friend, a man who at the time was working for me, had been driving his car when he had a complete nervous breakdown. He wrecked his car, and when the police came to try to take him to the hospital, he resisted. The police thought he was on drugs. They tried to subdue him. Well, my friend was pretty strong, so the officers responded in force as well. Two police officers and two ambulance drivers worked him over until I could hardly recognize him. I went down to the jail where they had placed my friend in a padded cell. I want to tell you that when I looked in that cell and saw my friend in that condition, I was really moved. I got him out of there and into a hospital where he needed to be. I don't

1. William Barclay, *The Gospel of John*, rev. ed. The Daily Study Bible Series 2 (Philadelphia: Westminster Press, 1975), 236–246.

blame the officers; my friend was resisting them and probably punching them. I'm sure they thought they were dealing with a criminal. And yet I can't help thinking they didn't need to go as far as they did in subduing him. I've never seen anyone beaten so severely. I could hardly recognize him. But you know, I'm sure that Jesus looked worse. I'm sure that my friend's beating was nothing compared to what Jesus endured.

John describes how Pilate had Jesus flogged even though he could find no fault in Him. Then he describes how, after the beating, the soldiers brought Him out and began making fun of Him. "You say You're a king? Well, if You're a king, you should be dressed like a king. You shouldn't be standing here naked! We can't let a king stand around with no clothes!" So they found a purple robe and pulled it on over His head. This robe was an "inner robe," one that was worn underneath the outer robe, and it probably came about to Jesus' waist. They laughed uproariously. This was a great joke! "Look at the king of the Jews!"

"Oh, but wait," they said, "a king needs a crown. Get Him a crown."

Someone twisted a couple of thorn branches into a crude circle and jammed it down on His head, pushing the long, sharp thorns deep into His scalp. They put a reed in His hand for a scepter and fell down in front of Him, laughing and mocking and crying out, " 'Hail, King of the Jews!' " (John 19:3). Then they spit on Him and hit Him with their fists. What a picture! The King of kings being mocked and mistreated.

After the soldiers had had their fun, they got down to business. Pilate delivered Jesus to them for crucifixion. "So they took Jesus and led Him away" (verse 16). They put the cross on His back and began the procession to "a place called the Place of a Skull, which is called in Hebrew, Golgotha, where they crucified Him" (verses 17, 18).

Now, you've seen pictures of Jesus carrying the cross—two heavy timbers in the shape of the letter *t*. But that's not exactly how it was. The one condemned to be crucified carried only the cross member, the top part of the cross, a piece of timber somewhere between six and eight feet long. That was still a heavy load. His arms would be spread out, and the crosspiece would be chained across his back. Around his neck was a placard on which was written his crime, the reason he was being executed. This sign had two purposes. First, it was there so that people could see it and know why this person was being executed. We don't publicly execute people anymore; we hide that away. But back then they wanted people to see and to know why this person was being executed. So they wrote his crime on a board and placed it around his neck. Later, it would be nailed to his cross. Second, his crime was displayed around his neck in case someone knew of some evidence that had not been brought out at his trial. If so, that person could come forward and testify on behalf of the condemned; there was still a chance of appeal even on the way to execution.

To us, the cross is a beautiful thing. We engrave it on our pulpits and on the ends of our pews. We carry it on the little zippers of our Bibles; some people wear a little cross on their lapels or around their necks. We think of the cross today as something beautiful and dear. But, my friend, the cross was simply a means of execution. It would be like wearing a hangman's noose or a little electric chair on your lapel. Because Jesus died on a cross, the cross has come to have deep meaning for Christians. But it had no meaning prior to that. None whatsoever.

Three men died on crosses on Golgotha that afternoon. There could have been a thousand, and none of them could have died for you—except Jesus Christ, the King of kings and Lord of lords. He walked to the place of execution, carrying the crosspiece to which He would soon be nailed. People jeered at Him and spit on Him as He passed. You remember how He had to have help carrying the heavy piece of timber. Back during His ministry on earth He had spoken of taking up one's cross. "Take up your cross, your burden, and follow Me," He said (see Matthew 16:24). Someone had to help Jesus carry His cross. Simon came along and helped Jesus carry His cross (see Matthew 27:32; Mark 15:21; Luke 23:26). And Someone has to help us carry ours as well. Just as Simon came along and helped Jesus, so Jesus helps you and me to carry our crosses today.

Jesus went to the cross, and He died. There was no doubt that He was dead. As it grew later and later on that Friday afternoon, the Jews began to worry about the bodies of these three men staying on the cross over Sabbath. They were anxious for them to die and get it over with.

> [So] the Jews asked Pilate that their legs might be broken, and that they might be taken away. Then the soldiers came and broke the legs of the first and of the other who was crucified with Him [Jesus]. But when they came to Jesus and saw that He was already dead, they did not break His legs. But one of the soldiers pierced His side with a spear, and immediately blood and water came out. And he who has seen has testified, and his testimony is true; and he knows that he is telling the truth, so that you may believe (John 19:31–35).

Now I don't understand all of the physical terminology, but as it has been explained to me, watery fluid can form in the sac around the heart. And when the soldier thrust a spear into Jesus' side, he pierced the sac surrounding His heart so that this fluid ran out. There was no doubt that Jesus was truly dead. Crucifixion was not a quick way to die; it took hours and hours—days sometimes. But when the soldiers came around to hasten the death of these three men on crosses, they found that Jesus was already dead. Undeniably dead. Jesus died quickly because of the weight of the guilt of the sins of the world that was pressing upon His heart—your sins and mine. Sin—that's what killed the Savior. Not the cross, but sin.

"Then they took the body of Jesus, and bound it in strips of linen with the spices, as the custom of the Jews is to bury. Now in the place where He was crucified there was a garden, and in the garden a new tomb in which no one had yet been laid. So there they laid Jesus" (verses 40–42).

Without the death of Jesus, we have nothing. The great point of the Crucifixion is that He died and shed His blood for you and me. We don't like to talk about blood and death. But Jesus' death on the cross is the most unselfish, the most beautiful thing that has ever taken place in our world. Because He was willing to die, we can live. Because He was willing to die; we have eternal life. Throughout eternity, the cross will be something that will unfold and become more wonderful and more beautiful the more we understand it. For now, it's enough to accept it, to thank Jesus for what He did there, and to accept Him as our Savior.

Chapter 8 — John 20

HE IS RISEN

Dr. Frank Morrison was a lawyer by profession, but he was a skeptic by nature. He decided that he would do the very best he could to destroy the "myth" of Jesus' resurrection. Dr. Morrison had been a student of German higher criticism, a theological school of thought that began from a position that the Bible had been written by human beings just as any other book. These higher critics looked at such questions as What were the literary sources behind the different sections of a book in the Bible? What influences had caused the book to be written? Was there internal consistency within the book? And they felt free to raise these questions, because they started from the position that the Bible was not divinely inspired, but had been written just as any other historical document was written.

Dr. Frank Morrison belonged to this school of German higher critical thought about the Bible. He was a man who was well known in the intellectual circles of his day. He had been a student of Thomas Huxley, who was a disciple of Charles Darwin. So Dr. Morrison decided to pull together all the evidence he could find from the Bible, history, and archaeology, and write a book that would destroy what he considered to be the myth of Jesus' resurrection from the dead. He began his research, but about halfway through his task, he threw up his hands in defeat. You see, although he had amassed all the evidence he could to destroy the validity of Jesus' resurrection—to dismiss it as a mere idle story—the more he studied, the more he became convinced that it was true! That Jesus really had risen from the dead! Instead of destroying this "myth" as he had set out to do, Dr. Morrison ended up accepting it completely. "I could not finish my book," he said, "because I now believe." Instead, he wrote another book, a totally different one than the book he set out to write. His book, *Who Moved the Stone?* is a great monument of affirmation and proof for Jesus' resurrection.

A lot of people have tried to debunk the resurrection of Jesus. Some say that Jesus never really died. My great-uncle, back in the 1930s (before I was born, by the way), became quite ill. I remember the story well because our family used to talk about it often. The family believed he was poisoned—either accidentally or on purpose—by some food he ate. He was kind of a character, and some people might not have been sorry to see him die! Anyway, the family took him to the hospital, where the doctors worked on him. They worked for quite a while, but they finally gave up and pronounced him dead. They put him in a little room and covered him up with a sheet. Someone called his sister, who was my grandmother. She was a strong, dynamic woman. She lost her husband when she was in her early thirties and was left with six children. After her husband died, she never had another date, never looked at another man. She didn't have time. She was a working person. She worked until she owned her own business, and then she operated that business until she was eighty-six years old!

My grandmother came to the hospital and asked, "Where is he?" They showed her the little room where they had put him. She went into the room and came back out. "I don't believe he's dead," she declared.

"He's dead," the doctor replied. "I pronounced him dead, and know a dead person when I see one."

She said, "I think he's alive. Did you pump his stomach?"

"Well, no, I didn't pump his stomach."

"Why didn't you pump his stomach?" she demanded. "You said he died of poison, something he ate. Why didn't you pump his stomach?"

She convinced an intern to help her, and they went back into that room where her brother was, and they revived him. He lived to the seventies. I don't mean he was in his seventies; I mean he lived until sometime in the 1970s. I don't know how old he was when he died. The point is he wasn't dead. The doctor thought he was dead, but he really wasn't.

I heard of an experience of a young man in Long Beach, California, who had an accident on a horse and was taken to an emergency room. He, too, was pronounced dead, and his mother donated a number of his organs—his eyes and a lot of other organs. The doctor came to get his eyes and was preparing for the surgery, when the young man opened his eyes! He wasn't dead, after all! He had been pronounced dead, but he wasn't.

So, some people have thought and have tried to prove that Jesus wasn't really dead. Now, remember that the Roman soldiers knew about death and dead people. It was their job to kill people. Of course, doctors also know about death and dead people, and yet doctors can be wrong—as we have just seen. Roman soldiers could be wrong too. These Roman soldiers wanted to be sure; this was the biggest crucifixion they had ever been involved with. So, as we saw in the last chapter, one of them took a spear and drove it into Jesus' side, and water and blood came out—sure evidence that Jesus was truly dead.

Those who argue that Jesus wasn't really dead also say that His disciples helped conceal that fact and helped their Master fake His death and resurrection. In chapter 19 of his Gospel, John says that Nicodemus and Joseph of Arimathea prepared a hundred pounds of spices. They took down Jesus' body and "bound it in strips of linen with the spices, as the custom of the Jews is to bury" (verse 40). Jesus died about three o'clock in the afternoon, so there was still time before sunset that Friday to prepare His body for burial. Now, if Jesus' followers were trying to conceal the fact that He hadn't really died, if they were helping Him fake His death and resurrection, would these two followers—Nicodemus and Joseph of Arimathea—be the ones you would expect to be involved in a fake burial? You might expect something like that of Peter. You might not put it past him, as impulsive as he always was. But Nicodemus was one of the religious leaders of the Jews, a member of the Sanhedrin. Joseph was a "prominent council member" (Mark 15:43). It's difficult to imagine them involved in this kind of trickery. If you look at their backgrounds, that doesn't seem very likely.

In preparing His body for burial, they mixed spices—aloes and myrrh, the Bible says—into a kind of batter. Then they took long strips of linen about a foot wide and wrapped the body, placing the spice batter between the layers of linen as they wrapped it around and around the body. The result was almost like a mummy. They pulled the jaw closed and tied it shut with a napkin over the head. Jesus was dead; there was no question about it. The Roman soldiers knew He was dead. Those who had prepared His body knew He was dead.

They took him to the tomb and placed His body inside. Then the tomb was sealed with a large stone. Tombs in those days and in that place were designed almost like a cave, with a sort of slot across the front for a large stone to be rolled into place, closing the opening. This stone was too big for a single man to move. It would take several to roll it either backward or forward. In the case of Jesus' tomb, a couple of additional precautions were taken at the request of the Jewish leaders. They came to Pilate and said, " 'We remember, while He was still alive, how that deceiver said, "After three days I will rise." Therefore command that the tomb be made secure until the third day, lest His disciples come by night and steal Him away, and say to the people, "He has risen from the dead." ' . . . Pilate said to them, 'You have a guard; go your way, make it as secure as you know how.' So they went and made the tomb secure, sealing the stone and setting the guard" (Matthew 27:63–66). The Jewish leaders set a seal on the stone that closed Jesus' tomb, and on top of that, they assigned a group of soldiers to guard the tomb. They wanted to avoid anything that could be seen as a fulfillment of Jesus' prediction that He would rise from the dead on the third day.

What was the seal they placed on the stone? It was a cord placed across the stone and sealed with a Roman seal in wax. Yes, someone could break the seal and remove the cord. But let me tell you, when the Romans sealed something, it was going to stay sealed! No one was going to defy the Roman authority.

And on top of that, the soldiers were there to make sure Jesus' disciples didn't interfere, break the seal, and steal away their Master's body. The seal also ensured that the Roman soldiers couldn't somehow collude with Jesus' disciples to remove His body. It was very unlikely that such a thing would happen, of course. The soldiers were not believers in Jesus. They believed in one thing—and that was the authority of Rome. Besides, they had great disdain for the Jews. So it wasn't very likely that the soldiers would conspire with the disciples. But just in case they might, there was a big wax seal on the stone that would clearly show if anyone broke it to remove the stone.

But maybe a soldier would go to sleep while guarding the tomb. In the Medical Cadet Corps at what is now Southwestern Adventist University, I was first sergeant, because I had the loudest mouth. At least, I guess that's why I was chosen for that job. The first sergeant, by the way, wasn't the top man. We had a major and a captain and lots of lieutenants, all of whom were above the first sergeant. But the sergeant was the field man, the one out there with the troops. That was the job I liked. But if we found someone sleeping on guard duty, we used to give him a "hot foot." We'd stick a match in the guy's shoe or boot, light it, and walk away. He would be snoring, and then all of a sudden, the heat would hit him, and he came awake pretty quickly! The Romans had a different plan when a guard went to sleep. They set his clothes on fire! He didn't get a hot foot; he got the whole thing. We're talking about a loosely fitted garment that wasn't made out of some kind of flame-resistant polyester fabric that had received approval from a federal safety agency. Those tunics were made of natural fibers that really burned! Going to sleep on guard duty was a serious matter in the Roman army. So the soldiers that were detailed to guard Jesus' tomb took that assignment very seriously.

In light of all these factors, it's really difficult to believe that someone might have sneaked in and stolen away Jesus' body. Who would have done such a thing? His enemies? Would His enemies have stolen His body and taken it away? That wouldn't make sense, would it? Why would His enemies do something that would cause people to believe He had risen from the dead?

Would His friends have done it? They were afraid. The disciples had scattered, fearful for their own lives. And how could they have done it without some kind of collusion with the Roman guard? I don't think a reasonable person would have ever come up with a theory that would explain why or how either His enemies or His friends would have stolen Jesus' body from the tomb. The most believable explanation, the explanation that makes the most sense, is that Jesus rose from the dead just as He said He would. And that's the explanation that John gives us here in chapter 20 of his Gospel:

> Now on the first day of the week Mary Magdalene went to the tomb early, while it was still dark, and saw that the stone had been taken away from the tomb. The she ran and came to Simon Peter, and to the other disciple, whom Jesus loved, and said to them, "They have taken away the Lord out of the tomb, and we do not know where they have laid

Him." Peter therefore went out, and the other disciple, and were going to the tomb. So they both ran together, and the other disciple outran Peter and came to the tomb first. And he, stooping down and looking in, saw the linen cloths lying there; yet he did not go in. Then Simon Peter came, following him, and went into the tomb; and he saw the linen cloths lying there, and the handkerchief that had been around His head, not lying with the linen cloths, but folded together in a place by itself. Then the other disciple, who came to the tomb first, went in also; and he saw and believed. For as yet they did not know the Scripture, that He must rise again from the dead (verses 1–9).

The reactions of these first three persons who are aware that Jesus is no longer in the tomb ring true. Mary is bewildered. Jesus' body has disappeared; she assumes someone has moved it, but she has no idea where. Peter and John (he modestly refers to himself as the "other disciple") are excited. Mary's news seems too good to be true. They run to see for themselves. They see the linen cloths and the handkerchief lying there all neatly folded. The Bible says that John saw and he believed (see verse 8). That was his reaction. Impetuous Peter rushed inside the tomb, and I have no question whatsoever in my mind that he also believed. The Bible says that afterwards, Peter and John went away to their own homes (see verse 10).

Then Mary Magdalene returned to the tomb. She was crying. She saw two angels in white clothes who asked her why she was crying. She answered, " 'Because they have taken away my Lord, and I do not know where they have laid Him' " (verse 13). She didn't realize that these were angels.

Then, you remember, she turned around, and there was Jesus! Some people have wondered why it took Mary so long to see Jesus there at the tomb that Sunday morning. Well, I can think of two very good reasons. First, Mary was focused on the empty tomb. You know, we sometimes do that same thing. We look at the empty tomb rather than at the Lord. We focus on the problems, and when we do, we don't see Jesus.

Second, Mary didn't see the Lord because her eyes were filled with tears. This was a woman who was a very emotional person. In fact, her approach to life was pretty much based on feeling. She was the kind of person who was up one day and down the next. If she felt good, then everything was OK. If she didn't, then nothing was OK. She was guided by feelings. And you know something? That is the same way a lot of us Christians approach life. We are guided so much by our feelings. It's good to have emotions and feelings, but they are not necessarily reliable guides. Sometimes our feelings can lead us astray. We need to hold on to faith even when our feelings and emotions are in turmoil and disarray.

Sometimes people tell you, "You have to take care of the weaker brother." You know, I sometimes want to say to the weaker brother, "Grow up! Don't let your feelings make you weak! Be strong in the Lord! Trust in Him. You've been a weaker brother too long. You need to grow strong in the faith and trust in the Lord Jesus Christ!"

You can't let your feelings always control your relationship with Jesus. You don't do that with your job, do you? When the alarm clock goes off in the morning, you don't say, "I just don't feel like getting up and going to work this morning. I'm going to say in bed; some of the other people at work will cover for me this morning. Maybe I'll get up and come in to work sometime this afternoon if I feel like it." You don't do that. If you do, you may have had a lot of different jobs lately—and none of them have lasted very long! Because your employer isn't going to make allowances for your feelings. Why, then, do we let our feelings control our spiritual lives?

Mary was one who went by her feelings. She was also a "toucher." You know what I mean. "Touchers" are people who are always reaching out and taking your hand or patting your arm or shoulder. I'm not putting that down, by the way. It's just the way some people are. And that was how Mary was. She was a toucher. When she finally saw Jesus and recognized Him, she reached out to embrace Him. " 'Do not cling to Me,' " Jesus told her, " 'for I have not yet ascended to My Father' " (verse 17). The King James Version has Jesus tell her, "Touch me not." But "do not cling to Me" is more accurate. Mary didn't just touch Jesus, she was holding on to Him, clinging to Him.

There is a lot of meaning in what Jesus said. He was saying, "Mary, things are going to be different now following My resurrection. I'm not going to be around very long. You won't be able to see Me. You won't be able to touch Me physically like you're used to doing. From now on, you're going to have to cling to Me by faith and trust." And that's a completely different thing, isn't it? Like Mary, you and I have to learn to cling to Jesus by faith. We can't see Him; we can't touch Him physically. But He's here with us. We must cling to Him by faith and trust Him when He says, " 'I will never leave you nor forsake you' " (Hebrews 13:5).

Then there was the reaction of the other disciples, the ones that had gathered that same night to hide from the Jewish authorities. No doubt, by this time, they had heard about the empty tomb. Some of them probably believed that Jesus had risen from the dead; others probably didn't. But they were all afraid of the Jews. *What in the world are we going to do? Are we going to be next? What's going to happen now?* Then, all at once, Jesus appeared right there in the room with them even though the door was shut and locked! His resurrected body was real, but He also had some amazing abilities. One minute they were all by themselves; the next moment, Jesus was standing in their midst. "Shalom," He said to them. " 'Peace be with you.' When He had said this, He showed them His hands and His side. Then the disciples were glad when they saw the Lord" (John 20:19, 20). I think that has to be an understatement, don't you? I think they were more than glad. They must have been overjoyed and amazed. Their fear turned to delight; their sorrow to unbelievable joy. I can just imagine the questions they must have had.

But there was one disciple who wasn't there that night. "Now Thomas, called the Twin, one of the twelve, was not with them when Jesus came" (verse 24). We don't know why Thomas wasn't with the other disciples that night in the upper room, but he missed that wonderful event. The other disciples told him how Jesus had appeared to them. I'm sure they spared no detail in telling him about it.

How do you think Thomas felt when he heard that Jesus had come to see the rest of the disciples and he had missed it? Well, how would you feel? Disappointed? Hurt? Sorry for yourself? Upset? Jealous? I'm sure all those feelings surged through Thomas's heart.

Thomas was hurt at being left out. And so, he decided to disbelieve the whole thing. The other disciples thought they were so special? Well, he didn't think they had seen anything at all. They were just making it up—or else they were seeing things. " 'Unless I see in His hands the print of the nails, . . . and put my hand into His side, I will not believe,' " he declared. (verse 25).

Now, sometimes we like to put Thomas down for his attitude. We like to call him "Doubting Thomas." We say he should have believed what the other disciples told him even though he hadn't seen the risen Lord himself. But I say, "Let's not be so hard on Thomas. Let's be careful about putting him down." Even Jesus was gentle in His rebuke to Thomas.

Eight days after He appeared to all the disciples except Thomas, Jesus showed up again—and this time Thomas was there. Jesus told him, " 'Reach your finger here, and look at My hands; and reach your hand here, and put it into My side. Do not be unbelieving, but believing' " (verse 27). Thomas had said he wouldn't believe unless he could see for himself. And Jesus gave him that opportunity. He rebuked him gently.

Different people need different things. Thomas was a man who needed facts. Back in John 14, when Jesus was talking to His disciples the night before His arrest in the garden, He said, " 'I go to prepare a place for you. . . . And where I go you know, and the way you know' " (John 14:2, 4). And Thomas replied, " 'Lord, we do not know where You are going, and how can we know the way?' " (verse 5). Thomas's typical reaction was to demand facts, to question, to want an explanation that made sense. Thomas was the kind of person who needed to understand all the ins and outs and the reasons. His whole philosophy was "proving is believing." He was probably a melancholy personality, the kind of person with a lot on his mind and always searching for the answers to things. Thomas was like the person in your classes in high school or college who was always up there near the top when it came to grades. He wanted things to make sense; he wanted to understand how things worked. Once he had the facts, then he would believe. There is a little bit of Thomas in all of us. We want evidence; we want facts. And that's not a bad thing necessarily. There should be facts on which our faith is based. If you subtract facts from faith, you'll have a weak faith with no solid foundation. There must be facts involved in faith.

But faith can't be *all* facts—or it wouldn't be faith. There has to be something more to faith. If you try to add sight to faith, you'll end up with doubts. And that's what Jesus pointed out to Thomas. He said, " 'Thomas, because you have seen Me, you have believed. Blessed are those who have not seen and yet have believed' " (John 20:29). The only way to have real faith is to add nothing to it except biblical truth—those things that the Bible affirms as true and trustworthy. And, my friend, if you do that, trusting in the Lord Jesus Christ and His sacrifice, you'll have the kind of faith that leads to life eternal. You'll have a believing faith. You'll have life in His name.

Today, you can choose to believe in Jesus Christ. You don't have to put your finger in the scars of His hand. You can believe without seeing Him physically, because He is always with you. In spite of all the critics who have tried to pile up facts and evidence to refute the truth of Jesus' crucifixion and resurrection, they have never done so successfully. Not one. Not once. Critics come and go; they fall by the wayside. But the great truth of Jesus' life, death, and resurrection remains forever. It continues to live and grow in the hearts of believers all over the world.

I challenge you to believe. I challenge you to say, "Lord, I don't understand everything about the plan of salvation. I don't understand all there is to know about Your life and death and resurrection. But I choose to believe. I choose to accept You as my Lord and Savior."

That's what the disciples did. They certainly didn't understand everything that was happening around them. They didn't understand Jesus' resurrection—or the full meaning of His death. But they chose to believe. Even Thomas. And that's what you and I need to do too.

Chapter 9 — John 21

NEVER GIVE UP

"After these things Jesus showed Himself again to the disciples at the Sea of Tiberias . . . Simon Peter, Thomas called the Twin, Nathanael of Cana in Galilee, the sons of Zebedee, and two others of His disciples were together. Simon Peter said to them, 'I am going fishing.' They said to him, 'We are going with you also' " (John 21:1–3).

There have been times I wanted to go fishing. I remember when I was a young man and Fordyce Detamore, Roger Holley, and Ray Turner came to Tyler, Texas, to hold evangelistic meetings. All three of these men are dead now, but they are classic names in Adventist evangelism. It was during the meetings that they held in Tyler that I really decided to follow the Lord. I hadn't been headed in that direction at all before those meetings. It was these three men who attracted me and impressed me as individuals as much as the message they preached, because I had grown up knowing the message. And one of the main things that attracted me to those preachers was that I saw that they were real men. Pastor Turner came to the meetings one night all sunburned. I asked him, "Where have you been?"

"I've been fishing," he answered.

"Do you mean preachers go fishing?" I wanted to know.

"Well," he said, "they don't always admit it to everyone, but yes, preachers do go fishing. Don't tell everybody."

So since then, I've told everybody about Elder Turner going fishing! You know, there's nothing more relaxing than fishing, is there? Sometimes you don't even want to bait your hook; you just throw out your line and sit in the boat! You don't care whether or not you catch anything. In fact, you're hoping you don't catch anything! You don't want to disturb the peace. Fishing is just something that gives you a reason for being out in the boat and getting away from it all. There's nothing wrong with going fishing. Don't ever get it in your head that there is, because there isn't. But there *is* something wrong with going fishing when God wants you to be somewhere else. When God has a place for you and you make up your mind that you're going to be somewhere else, that you're going to do what *you* want to do, then there's a problem.

Matthew says that Jesus had appointed a certain mountain where He would meet with His disciples following His resurrection (see Matthew 28:16). I don't know what was going through Peter's mind. Maybe he went to that mountain and hung around for a while and got tired of waiting. Maybe Jesus didn't show up as quickly as Peter expected Him to. Peter always was kind of impetuous. Maybe he got to wondering about the future. *What's going to happen to us now? The Lord has been providing for us the last two, three years; now it looks like we're going to have to start taking care of ourselves. He isn't going to be around to feed us like He did the five thousand that time. I'm tired of waiting around this mountain. I'm going to go back to doing what I know best. I'm going fishing.* The other disciples said, "We're going with you."

It's amazing, isn't it, how some people seem to be natural leaders? They say something, and it just seems to happen. A while back, I was with a good friend who was telling me of an experience that took place in some evangelistic meetings he was holding. Now, several mentally challenged people were coming to these meetings. They looked normal, and no one would have guessed at first that they had problems. One, in particular, would come to the meetings dressed nicely, wanting to help. The people would give him something to do, but really he wasn't mentally able to carry out even a little job. But he got to be good friends with the evangelist—the man who was telling me this story.

One day, right at noon, my evangelist friend came by the auditorium where he was holding meetings each evening. He came to check on something. When he got to the auditorium, here was this man out in the middle of the street right in front of the auditorium. He had a walkie-talkie in his hand, and every car that came by, he was directing into the parking lot beside the auditorium! My friend said that when he got there, the parking lot was half full. People were sitting there in their cars, looking around, wondering, *What do we do now?* Some were leaving out the back, but most of them were just sitting there confused, because this nice-looking man wearing a suit and holding a walkie-talkie had motioned them into the parking lot. He looked like he knew what he was doing. He looked like he was in charge.

My evangelist friend jumped out of his car and ran over to the man. "What are you doing?" he asked.

"Parking cars."

"Well, put that walkie-talkie away and get out of the street," he told him. "You're going to get run over!" My friend was finally able to persuade him that it wasn't meeting time and that everyone who came down the street wasn't coming to the meetings and didn't need to be in the parking lot.

You know, if you have a walkie-talkie in your hand and act like you know what you're doing, you can get people to do almost anything! But aside from that, this man who was mentally challenged had such a commanding presence about him that people just naturally did what he told them to do. Peter was not mentally challenged. However, he was a leader with a commanding presence; when he said, "I'm going fishing," the other disciples said, "We're going too."

So they went down to the lake and got in the boat and started fishing. The Bible says that they fished all night—and caught nothing at all (see John 21:3). You can't tell me that that was accidental. I believe the Lord re-routed every fish in the Sea of Galilee that night, so that the fish didn't come anywhere near the disciples' boat. They fished everywhere and caught nothing.

Now, there is a process, a sequence, that we are seeing in what is happening here. First, there is *self-reliance,* a dependence on one's own efforts. Self-reliance brings about the second item in the sequence, which is *disobedience.* What the disciples were doing was not necessarily wrong in itself. Fishing is not a sin—unless God has told you to do something else. If something is not what God wants you to do, then it's wrong even though it is not sinful in and of itself. That thing might not be sin for anyone else, but it is for you if God has something else for you to do. Disobedience, in turn, brings *failure* and *disappointment.* And the final step in the sequence is *the loss of an intimate fellowship with the Lord Jesus Christ.* Self-reliance, disobedience, failure and disappointment, and the loss of an intimate fellowship with the Lord Jesus Christ: that's what Peter and the other disciples were experiencing as they went out fishing on the lake.

This is the exact opposite of the progression that God wants for us. That progression begins with relying on Him and obeying Him—and it ends in a close relationship with Him. *Obedience* is a word that we've largely taken out of our vocabulary today. It's a word that we don't really like very much. But nonetheless, obedience is very much the essence of a trusting relationship with Jesus. Obedience brings about success and happiness and results in an intimate fellowship with the Lord Jesus Christ. It's like a circle, with one thing leading to the next, around and around. Now, if the circle gets out of balance, we lose the fellowship. This doesn't mean that we're lost. In our Christian experience, we often find ourselves in and out of this close fellowship. We may be going one direction for a while and then the other direction. Remember, we are not saved or lost by the momentary direction we may be going. We're saved by the commitment we have made to the Lord Jesus to accept Him as our Lord and Savior. If you have sincerely given your life Jesus, then you are born again.

But the Christian life is a matter of relationship. As you become closer and closer to the Lord, you are going to find that your fellowship with Him is more and more one of harmony. You will begin to see a progression in your life that is more a matter of divine effort than it is of self-effort. Success in life depends on doing and being what God wants you to do and be. Success is not measured by your title or standing in the community or how much money you make. You can have a lot of money and still do exactly what God does *not* want you to do. Maybe you're making a lot of money because the devil is blessing you in order to keep you from being what God wants you to be.

If you are going to enter into the fullness of the life that Christ wants for you, you will need to discover exactly what it is that He wants you to do—and then you will need to enter into that experience and walk with Him. Every single one of us—no matter what your occupation is in this life—should also have a ministry. Whether you work for the city road maintenance department or you're a surgeon, whether you're a housewife or a business executive, you should also have a spiritual ministry. Whatever you do in life, make sure you put Christ first. Then you can enter into whatever you are doing with all your heart and know that He is leading and directing your life. You know, one of the biggest problems most of us have is that either we love our jobs too much or we hate them. There just doesn't seem to be any place in between. We're either obsessed with our jobs and spend way too much time working or we dread hearing the alarm clock every morning and having to go to work again. What we need is balance. We need priorities in life—priorities that put Christ first.

That's what the disciples needed. Here they were—fishing—when they were supposed to be at the mountain meeting Jesus. And they weren't having much success catching fish either! "When the morning had now come, Jesus stood on the shore; yet the disciples did not know that it was Jesus. Then Jesus said to them, 'Children, have you any food?' They answered Him, 'No' " (John 21:4, 5).

Why didn't they recognize Jesus? Why, at least, didn't

they recognize His voice when He called to them?

They didn't recognize Him because they weren't where they were supposed to be. They weren't in an intimate fellowship with Him. They had gone off fishing when they should have been on the mountain. They had voluntarily separated themselves from Him.

Sometimes, we don't recognize God's voice to us because we are not where He wants us to be. We're too far from Him. We don't recognize His leading in our lives because we aren't close enough to Him in our experiences and in our prayers.

When the disciples admitted they hadn't been able to catch a thing all night, the Man on the shore told them, " 'Cast the net on the right side of the boat, and you will find some' " (verse 6). Now if I had been in that boat, I would probably have replied, "Do you think we've been fishing only on the left side of the boat all night? We've been fishing on the right and the left and everywhere else." But the disciples did what this Man told them to do. I think they must have remembered something that had happened three and half years earlier at the beginning of Jesus' ministry (see Luke 5:1–11). In response to the Stranger's suggestion, the disciples wearily lowered the net over the right side of the boat. And "they were not able to draw it in because of the multitude of fish" (verse 6).

Now Jesus didn't really need to ask them lower the net on the right side of the boat. He could have skipped the net altogether and had the fish just jump into the boat with the disciples. He could have had the fish jump into the boat already cleaned and ready for the frying pan, for that matter! But He didn't. He told the disciples to lower the net on the right side of the boat. Jesus may work miracles, but He always involves human beings as well. You remember when Gideon and his men came down upon the enemy, they cried out, " 'The sword of the LORD and of Gideon' " (Judges 7:20). Now, if you have the sword of the Lord, why do you need Gideon's sword? You see, the Lord put the two together. The Lord wants to link up with us to bring true spiritual success into our lives. When the disciples did what the Lord asked them to do, there were so many fish in the net that they couldn't haul it in! That's the result of God's miracle-working power and human obedience.

When that happened, John (he calls himself the "disciple whom Jesus loved") exclaimed to Peter, " 'It is the Lord!' " (John 21:7). Now, Peter had been fishing in his underwear—or maybe not even that! As soon as he heard John say, "It's the Lord!" Peter hastily pulled on his cloak and jumped overboard, swimming as hard as he could for the shore! You'd think the cloak would get all waterlogged and make it hard to swim. I've heard people say that Peter got so excited when he realized who was on shore that he wasn't thinking clearly, and that's why he put on clothes before jumping into the water. I don't believe that at all. I think Peter had so much respect for the Lord that he didn't want to show up on shore without his clothes on.

Peter couldn't wait; he was overwhelmed with a desire to be with the Lord. The others came to shore in the boat, dragging the net full of fish alongside, since they weren't able to lift it into the boat. So many times we see things about Peter that we criticize and fault him for. Yet at other times, we see qualities in Peter that we wish we had. Peter had such a desire to be with Jesus that he wasn't going to wait even a moment. He jumped right into the water to get to shore as quickly as he could. The Bible says they were only two hundred cubits from land—about a hundred yards. It wasn't very far, but it was too far for Peter to wait! Don't you like that about Peter? Don't you wish you had more of that kind of a longing to be with Jesus? I do.

And by the time Peter, and then the boat, came to shore, Jesus already had breakfast ready! I wish I could see a video of that! I wish I could see it as well as read about it, don't you? I have a theory—it's strictly a personal theory only—but if we can have television signals that can record events anywhere in the world and beam them live into our homes twenty-four hours a day, then I believe the Lord is able to re-create and replay scenes from the past as well. I believe that sometime in eternity, we may have the opportunity to view some of the important scenes from Jesus' life. Wouldn't you love to do that? I would. The Sea of Galilee is one of my favorite spots in the whole world. Not only would I love to see the video of Jesus and the disciples having breakfast beside the Sea of Galilee, I'd love (sometime during eternity) to have breakfast with Him and some of my friends beside the Sea of Galilee in the earth made new. Wouldn't that be something?

When the disciples got to shore, Jesus already had some fish cooking. He had some bread. By this He was telling them: "I am still your Provider. I am still the Source of all you need. You don't have to face life alone. Just because I'm not going to be with you physically any longer, doesn't mean that I won't be with you all the time through the Spirit." And that's true for us as well. Jesus is your Provider. He is the Source of all you need. He's with you always through the Holy Spirit. Your employer is not your provider. Jesus is—the One who fixed breakfast for the disciples there beside the Sea of Galilee. The One who filled their net to overflowing after they had not been able to catch a single fish all night. We don't need to worry whether Jesus will take care of us.

By the way, the Bible even tells us how many fish were in that net—153 (see verse 11). That was a big haul for Peter, Andrew, James, and John Incorporated, successful fishing firm!

When they had gone back to fishing, they were turning away from the call that Jesus had given them when He called them to be " 'fishers of men' " (Matthew 4:19). We have always thought of them as poor fishermen, however when archaeologist Harold Weiss led the excavation team that discovered Peter's house in Capernaum they found a large home, not the hut of a poor man. Malcolm Cartier, a well-known tour guide and scholar in Israel, claims that these men had developed a very successful export business, exporting fish by the barrel to Rome where they received top dollar. There are other sources that claim that Zebedee, the father of James and John, was also a very successful fisherman, who sold fish to the residence of Caiaphas. This is why John and some other disciples like Peter were given access to the residence when Christ was brought there the night of His trial.

It would make sense that Christ would call hard-working, creative individuals to spread the gospel to the world, wouldn't it? I don't think that Christ was against their being in the fishing business, just as long as their main business was spreading the gospel! He later used a tent maker by the name of Paul to reach a large portion of the then-known world!

Jesus wants to be a very real part of your life today. He doesn't want to be just Someone that you sing about and pray to on Sabbath morning. He wants to be your constant Companion. And He will be—if you let Him.

"So when they had eaten breakfast, Jesus said to Simon Peter, 'Simon, son of Jonah, do you love Me more than these?' " (John 21:15). What does Jesus mean by "these"? Most of us have thought that He meant more than the other disciples. But careful study indicates that Jesus was talking about the fish, the fishing business that they were involved with, making money, putting temporal things first. Remember, most of these disciples joined Him, not to spread the gospel but because they thought that He was going to overthrow Rome and set up His kingdom on this earth! "He [Peter] said to Him, 'Yes, Lord; You know that I love You.' He [Jesus] said to him, 'Feed My lambs' " (verse 15). Here we see Jesus beginning the beautiful process of reinstating Peter. Peter, you see, was totally out of fellowship with the Master. He had denied Jesus with cursing and swearing. He had denied that he was a follower of Jesus. Of course, Peter was terribly, terribly sorry. He had repented. Jesus knew that. Peter knew that. But for the sake of the other disciples, Jesus needed to have Peter formally go through a process of reinstatement. And Peter needed it too. Peter needed to be brought face-to-face with the awful thing he had done and the tremendous love and forgiveness of Jesus.

Jesus waited until they had finished eating breakfast. There are a lot of subjects that should never be brought up until you are finished eating! A lot of subjects that have destroyed some very good meals. Has that ever happened at your house? Sometimes it's best to wait until after the meal is over to bring up a touchy subject. And that's what Jesus did. Something had to be dealt with in front of all the disciples, because they were all aware of the situation. But Jesus waited until the time was right, and then He dealt with the situation firmly but gently.

Notice in verse 15 that Jesus calls Peter, " 'Simon, son of Jonah.' " He doesn't call him *Peter*. He doesn't call him *Cephas,* "the Rock." He goes all the way back to the old name, because Peter had gone all the way back. He had left preaching; he was back to the fishing business just as he had been when Jesus had first found him. " 'Simon, son of Jonah,' " He asked, " 'Do you love Me?' " Three times Jesus asked Peter that question. Why? Do you remember how many times Peter had denied Jesus? Three times, wasn't it? So Jesus has Peter affirm three times that he loves Him. And when the reinstating process is finished, Jesus says, " 'Follow Me' " (verse 19). He repeats the original call He made to Peter to leave his nets and all that meant and follow Him.

Skip forward a few weeks. We're still in Jerusalem. Jesus has returned to heaven. The Holy Spirit has just been poured out on the disciples in full measure on the Day of Pentecost. There is a great stir throughout the city; word is spreading like wildfire that something very unusual is happening down near the center of town. People begin heading that direction. Soon hundreds are gathered, and before long, the crowd swells to thousands. Something is happening that the people can't quite grasp. Several Galileans are standing around, speaking to groups of people. And the people are hearing them in their own languages. Now, there is some question among Bible students about whether the disciples were actually speaking foreign languages or whether they were speaking their usual Aramaic, but the people were hearing and understanding them in a number of different languages. Whichever it was, it was a strange, miraculous event that was taking place. "They're drunk!" someone shouts. "No," responds someone else. "They can't be drunk; it's too early in the day!"

All of a sudden, out of all this turmoil, excitement, and commotion, one man stands up. The Rock—Peter, fully restored as a disciple and apostle. And he preaches a sermon like he's never preached before and like he'll never preach again. God's Holy Spirit comes down upon him with even greater power, driving home his message as Peter preaches about the life, death, and resurrection of Jesus Christ, his Lord and Master. And as Peter speaks, God's Spirit speaks through him to the hearts of his listeners, and three thousand people decide to accept Jesus Christ that day! Can you imagine the excitement and the thrill? That little band of Jesus' followers became vastly larger overnight! You can read this story in Acts 2.

I don't know what went through Peter's mind at a time like that. But he must have realized that there was absolutely no question that the Holy Spirit had used him in a mighty way that day. He must have realized, if he hadn't earlier, that Jesus had forgiven his denials and had restored him to full fellowship. He must have been humbled by the realization that he was an instrument in the hand of the Holy Spirit to bring about a mighty work for God's kingdom.

When we look at Peter's experience, we can see how he struggled, as we so often do, to stay close to the Master—struggled and failed and then pressed on through to repentance and restoration and an even closer fellowship with the Lord. As Peter knew—and as we know—the Christian life often involves struggle. We don't enjoy struggles, but they are a major part of life. And struggle is an important part of Christian growth. The greatest struggle is not a struggle of works; the greatest struggle is the struggle to become one with Jesus Christ. It's a struggle of faith. The enemy will destroy you if he can. So you have to hold on to Jesus. You are not alone in your struggles; Jesus is there with you, just as He was there with Peter.

The struggles in the Christian life are like the weights in bodybuilding. It's the resistance to the weights that builds muscle and endurance and strength. Christ wants to build your faith; He wants it to grow and become strong. Struggles can help that process along.

Of course, struggles can also tear down faith. Whether struggle builds your faith or tears it down depends on whether you allow Jesus to come into your life and be a part of the struggle with you. That's what makes the difference. And that's what Peter did. He may have denied the Lord under the pressure of the moment, but he never really shut Jesus out of his life. No matter how often he struggled and failed, he always loved the Lord and wanted to be in fellowship with Him. That's how Peter dealt with failure in his life—by clinging to Jesus no matter what.

When Jesus was reinstating Peter, He asked, " 'Simon, son of Jonah, do you love Me?' " And Peter answered, " 'Lord, You know all things; You know that I love You' " (John 21:17). "You know my heart, Lord," Peter was saying. "You can see inside me; You know that I love You in spite of the fact that I denied You three times."

I'm so glad that Jesus knows our hearts, because sometimes my actions have said to Him, "I don't love You." That's what my actions have said, but I'm glad He knows my heart. Sometimes your actions have cried out, "God, I don't love You," but He knows your heart, and He knows that you do love Him. Oh, my friend, don't ever give up on Jesus! In the darkest hour of the night, when you've disappointed Him, remember that you can never deny Him more than Peter did. And He forgave Peter. His forgiveness is so great that He can forgive and restore you.

That's the message of John's Gospel—God's great love for us as shown in the life, death, and resurrection of Jesus Christ. " 'For God so loved the world that He gave His only begotten Son, that whoever believes in Him should not perish but have everlasting life' " (John 3:16). God loves you. Jesus loves you. The question is, Do you love God? Do you love the Lord Jesus Christ? Can you answer with Peter, " 'Lord, You know all things; You know that I love You' " (John 21:17)?

SELECTED BIBLIOGRAPHY

Barclay, William. *The Gospel of John.* Rev. ed. The Daily Study Bible Series 2. Philadelphia: Westminster Press, 1975.

Boice, James Montgomery. *The Gospel of John: An Expositional Commentary.* Grand Rapids, Mich.: Zondervan Publishing House, 1985.

Bruce, F. F. *The Gospel of John.* Grand Rapids, Mich.: William B. Eerdmans Publishing, 1983.

Godet, Frederic Louis. *Commentary on John's Gospel.* Reprint, Grand Rapids, Mich.: Kregel Publications, 1980.

MacArthur, John. *John 12-21.* The MacArthur New Testament Commentary. Chicago: Moody Publishers, 2008.

Scott, W. Frank. *The Preacher's Complete Homiletic Commentary on the Gospel According to St. John.* Grand Rapids, Mich.: Baker Book House, 1986.

White, Ellen G. *The Desire of Ages.* Mountain View, Calif.: Pacific Press® Publishing Association, 1940.

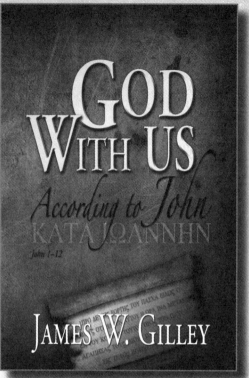
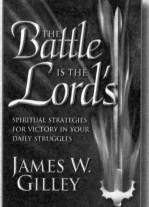

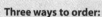